*Handwritten inscription:*
Deborah —
Enjoy the
book + often, hopefully,
you'll watch some
magical movie
moments by Ford
& Company.
Bill L
6/19/13

# *Lest We Forget:*
# *The John Ford Stock Company*

## Bill Levy

BearManor
Media

Albany, Georgia

Published in the USA by:

BearManor Media

P.O. Box 1129

Duncan, OK 73534-1129

www.BearManorMedia.com

ISBN 1-59393-236-7

Design and layout by Allan T. Duffin

Printed in the United States of America

*This book is dedicated to the quintessential Fordian, Tag Gallagher, whose scholarly work on John Ford has expanded our understanding of an extremely complex and enigmatic director, legend, and man.*

# Table of Contents

# Prologue

In his delightful 1994 book on his experiences as a member of John Ford's stock company, Harry Carey Jr. aptly used three words in the title to describe Ford's troupe: "Company of Heroes." This phrase captures the essence of Ford's ensemble of movie stars, character actors, and bit players who, in countless "Fordian moments," courageously exposed themselves to the world by revealing not only the heroic traits of the sure and the brave, but also an individual's weaknesses, vanities, and vulnerabilities.

In a conversation to newspaper reporters at the conclusion of *Fort Apache* (1948), Kirby York (John Wayne) talks about his fellow officers and troopers who have died in battle. He may just as well be speaking about the "regulars" of John Ford's stock company: "… they'll keep on living as long as the regiment lives…. The faces may change, the names, but they're there; they're the regiment, the regular army, now and fifty years from now."

# Acknowledgments

I am appreciative of the aid all of the following individuals provided me in writing this book.

Bear Manor Media publisher, Ben Ohmart and his shotgun guard, Sandy Grabman, were extremely positive in their support for this project. I also want to thank Bear Manor's Patricia Hanson and Annette Lloyd for their editing and Allan Duffin for the book design and typesetting.

Movie experts James Robert Parish and Anthony Slide gave me constant inspiration, advice, valuable contacts, and guidance. As they did with my first Ford book, Tag Gallagher and John Ford's grandson, Dan Ford, generously shared their encyclopedic knowledge of John Ford lore.

April Lane, the webmaster of the website, *Directed by John Ford*, and independent film director Mark Poisella continually offered encouragement and suggestions. Film scholars Robert M.

Fells and William Darby were repeatedly helpful in sharing their expertise with me. Fordians Scott Eyman and Joseph McBride were also supportive of this endeavor.

I wish to thank Rebecca Cape, Head of Reference and Public Services at The Lilly Library at Indiana University as well as librarians Anna Arays and Carly Sentieri for all of their assistance in locating photographs and networking.

I wish to thank Howard and Ron Mandlebaum, Derek Davidson, and the rest of the staff at Photofest in New York for providing me with the majority of the photographs in this book.

Others who helped me in writing this book were June Beck; Jose and Lorraine Cintron; Gerriane Delaney; Jen Francis Dwyer; Marcia and Stephen Falk; Michael Falken; Andrew Fielding; Frank Fredo; Larry Friedlander; Adrienne, Gabi, Jason, and Jasper Housman; Russell Hoyer; Wally Hubert; Alison and Douglas Irvin; Karen Lonergan; Robin McNutt; Sandy Marco; Ted Michelfelder; Christopher Monroe; Mark Phelan; Cole, Grace, Heather, and Kevin Schaefer; Barbara and Robert Scola; and Robert Ullian.

Finally, I wish to thank the seven ladies in my life for their love and inspiration: Janice Allen, Marlene Falken, Marsha Feldman, Diana Levy, Haley Levy, Michelle Levy, and Julienne Marks.

# Introduction

"It is worth recalling the characteristics of a John Ford movie.... They include the breathtaking sense of location, the leading actors–Wayne, Fonda, Jimmy Stewart–and the strong stock company–Ward Bond, Victor McLaglen, Ben Johnson, Woody Strode, many others. Some of them grew up with Ford; some grew old with him."

—*Roger Greenspun*[1]

"Every Ford movie is filled with reverberation from another–which makes his use of the same players from year to year, decade to decade, so much more than just building 'a stock company'–and one film of his cannot really be looked at as separated from the rest."

—*Peter Bogdanovich*[2]

# Overview

John Ford (1894-1973) directed scores of memorable motion pictures that feature countless scenes that linger in one's memory. He is the only director to have won four Best Director Academy Awards, for *The Informer* (1935), *The Grapes of Wrath* (1940), *How Green Was My Valley* (1941), and *The Quiet Man* (1952). He helmed films for over fifty years, beginning in 1917. He was the first recipient of the American Film Institute's Life Achievement Award.

There have been many biographies and film studies of John Ford and his motion pictures. There has, however, never been a single volume devoted to the stock company of actors and actresses who worked for him, some continually, many intermittently, from his silent westerns of the 'teens to his final films of the 1960s. This book spotlights 112 members of Ford's fluid repertory company.

In a memorable scene in *She Wore a Yellow Ribbon* (1949), John Wayne's character, Captain Nathan Brittles, is retiring from the Army. When his troopers present him with a solid silver watch, he awkwardly puts on his glasses and reads the inscription on the back of the watch out loud: "To Capt. Brittles from C Troop. Lest we forget." A sentiment quite appropriate for Captain Brittles. And for John Ford's company of players.

This book has three goals. One is to answer the question, "Who is that actor or actress?" The second is to share with readers the history, achievements, and uniqueness of John Ford's stock company. The third goal is to illustrate the roles John Ford and his band of actors and actresses played in creating engaging characters with distinct personalities, whether in cameo appearances, bit parts, or starring performances.

Ford's stock company was a diverse group. Some were classically trained thespians, some were former vaudeville clowns, some were decorated combat veterans, some were Ivy League graduates, and some were cowboys. One player wrote three books on the Baha'i Faith religion; another boxed the heavyweight champion of the world to a draw; one eloped with Loretta Young when she was seventeen; one participated in the Yukon gold rush; a photograph of one player's ear is the club logo for a professional wrestling association; another taught Lucy how to jitterbug; one was a legendary undercover agent for the OSS in France during World War II; another was a member of the advisory board to the Bank of America concerning loans to the studios, and two players were rodeo world champions. All of them, from extras to character actors to leads, made substantial contributions to Ford's movie legacy.

Most of Ford's players were from the United States, but many were born in England, Scotland, and Ireland. A few came from such distant locales as Norway, Austria-Hungary, and Australia. The oldest (Jennie Lee) was born in 1848; the youngest (Patrick Wayne) in 1939. Some of these actors and actresses were well-known movie stars like John Wayne, Henry Fonda, and Maureen O'Hara. Others, like George O'Brien, Harry Carey, Jane Darwell, and John Qualen, are not as well remembered today, while players such as Jack Pennick, Harry Tenbrook, and Ruth Clifford have been forgotten by all but the most fervent Fordians.

For almost 100 years, John Ford and these actors and actresses have shared with movie audiences, (and later, thanks to television and various recording devices, viewers at home), countless special Fordian moments. These scenes and segments of scenes, with or without dialogue, capture an individual's true inner personality. Sometimes a character's humorous side is revealed; at other times, a person's private and often painful thoughts, sentiments, and memories are exposed.

The people portrayed by Ford's stock company might be society's outsiders, silly jesters, nosey biddies, old and young romantics, reluctant heroes, emotional cripples, sensitive brutes, loyal comrades-in-arms, protective matriarchs, practical mentors, self-serving politicians, callow youths, or grizzled veterans. Many were outcasts as described by film scholar Scott Eyman, "the drunks, the outlaws, the whores, the people who live on the fringes"—or as British-Australian novelist Nevil Shute described some of his characters, "plain and simple people like ourselves, doing the best we can with each job as it comes along." These individuals are so real that most audiences would agree with Ford scholar Tag Gallagher that, "it seems more appropriate to designate a character solely by the name of his personage, and almost never by the name of the actor." Many of these characters in Ford's films touch us by revealing their humanity through a wide variety of memorable scenes, be they poignant, comic, or Homeric. [3]

## A Brief History of the John Ford Stock Company

The genesis of John Ford's stock company began in Hollywood in 1914 when John Ford arrived from Maine to work as an apprentice for his brother, Francis, a famous actor and director of silent serials. Together with his lady fair, Grace Cunard, Francis had established a stock company of actors whom he was comfortable directing, as was the norm in the film industry at the time. For three years, John apprenticed for his brother, learning all the tricks of the moving picture trade and growing to appreciate making movies surrounded by cronies and colleagues who knew exactly what was expected of them. When John began directing his own films in 1917, he continued using Francis's system.

With some initial guidance and mentoring from the older actor, Harry Carey, Ford established his own family of players, and created a personal community with his own imposed rites and rituals. This group provided him with a sanctuary from outside interference and a place where he felt at ease and could focus on his craft.

During the late 'teens and early 1920s, Ford directed numerous silent westerns starring Harry Carey for Universal. Players like Hoot Gibson, Molly Malone, Vester Pegg, Duke R. Lee, Pete Morrison, J. Farrell MacDonald, Joe Harris, and Ed Jones knew how to work with Ford and one another, which suited Ford's relaxed directing style.

There might be small changes in casting here and there, various leading ladies might be introduced, but basically the group stayed together. The gang even bedded down and boarded at Carey's ranch with Harry's wife, Olive, as a kind of mother hen. If Carey was unavailable, Ford used one of the other company's players like Hoot Gibson or Ed Jones as his leading man. [4]

Ford moved to Fox in 1921 and continued to use his company throughout the 1920s. During the ten years he was under contract with Fox, Ford began hiring others who would be featured in his films for decades, such as his brother Francis, Frank Baker, Ruth Clifford, Dan Borzage, Jack Pennick, George O'Brien, Victor McLaglen, Ward Bond, Harry Tenbrook, and John Wayne.

In 1931, Ford negotiated a new contract with the slumping Fox that allowed him to work at other studios. When he did, he took many of his company with him and also added new members to his troupe. For example, when Ford directed *Arrowsmith* for Goldwyn in 1931, he brought along players Frank Baker, Ward

Bond, and James Marcus, and worked for the first time with John Qualen, who would eventually make nine Ford films over the next thirty-odd years.

In 1935, 20th Century absorbed Fox, forming 20th Century-Fox. It was here that Ford's stock company acquired new members using many of the studio's contracted actors and actresses. During the last half of the 1930s, Henry Fonda, Stepin Fetchit, Berton Churchill, and John Carradine joined his group of actors to form a solid foundation of familiar players. Over the next thirty years, the company was always fluid, occasionally taking in rookies while the veterans continued to contribute. A few actors were consistent participants but most members, for a variety of personal and professional reasons, appeared sporadically in Ford's films.

Other directors, such as Frank Capra and Preston Sturges, had their own stock companies, but the sheer longevity of Ford's company made Ford's unique. For example, Duke R. Lee was in *The Soul Herder* in 1917 and *My Darling Clementine* in 1946; J. Farrell MacDonald was in *Roped* in 1919 and *When Willie Comes Marching Home* in 1950; brother Francis was in *Action* in 1921 and *The Sun Shines Bright* in 1953, and Dan Borzage was in *The Iron Horse* in 1924 and *Cheyenne Autumn* in 1964.

There were other distinctive aspects to Ford's company. One was his use of silent movie actors and actresses long after their popularity had waned. The most famous was silent star Mae Marsh, who had bit roles in fourteen Ford productions beginning with *Drums Along the Mohawk* in 1939 and ending with *Donovan's Reef* in 1963. Ford once explained, "Ex-stars will, after all, give a better performance even in the smallest part than any casual extra would." He added, "...when I was starting out in this town, those people were kind to me. I want to repay a little of that if it's in my power."[5]

Another difference was Ford's "Bad Boy's List." If an actor made a suggestion, and Ford thought his authority was being challenged, it might be years–if ever–before the actor worked for John Ford again. Long time company member Frank Baker called this, "being put on ice." Ford ignored a bewildered John Wayne for several years during the 1930s, and never used Henry Fonda again after *Mister Roberts* in 1955. According to Harry Carey Jr., any little thing could get an actor placed on the "List." This happened to Harry Carey, George O'Brien, Harry Carey Jr., Ben Johnson, Pedro Armendariz, James Lilburn, and Andy Devine. During the filming of *Stagecoach* in 1938, Ford screamed at Devine, "You big tub of lard. I don't know why the hell I'm using you in this picture!" Devine immediately yelled back, "Because Ward Bond can't drive six horses." Ford didn't talk to Devine for six years and didn't use him in one of his movies until *Two Rode Together* (1961), over twenty years later. Ford would also angrily retaliate against anyone who he felt questioned his directional authority. Maureen O'Hara described this as being "put in the barrel": "You never wanted to find yourself in Mr. Ford's barrel, which meant you were on John Ford's list to be tortured, made fun of, and tormented." [6]

An additional facet of Ford's stock company was the use of music on the set to create a mood. Ford had learned this technique during his days directing silent westerns when it was standard practice in film production. For over forty years, Dan Borzage was on hand on the set with his accordion to relax the director with Ford's favorite hymns and songs like "Shall We Gather at the River," "Danny Boy," "Bringing in the Sheaves," "I'll Take You Home Again, Kathleen," and "The Monkeys Have No Tails in Zamboanga." Specific company members were welcomed with their own special Ford movie song; for example, "Red River Valley" from *The Grapes of Wrath* (1940) for Henry Fonda, "The Streets of

Laredo" from *3 Godfathers* (1948) for Harry Carey Jr., "Wagons West" from *Wagon Master* (1950) for Ward Bond, and "Marcheta" from *They Were Expendable* (1945) for John Wayne. The songs and voices of Stan Jones, Ken Curtis, "The Sons of the Pioneers," Maureen O'Hara, and Harry Carey Jr. added to the melodies and music pervading Ford's sets in and out of the studio. [7]

## Ford and his Players

John Ford has been universally celebrated for his visual eye, his deceptively simple but wise perspectives, his use of landscape as an essential element in his films, and for his facility to combine the personal and the epic, the tragic and the comedic, and the optimistic and the cynical in his narratives. But Ford has never been fully appreciated for his ability to draw exceptional performances from his actors.

If Academy Awards and nominations indicate superior acting, it should be noted that John Ford directed ten different actors, five women and five men, to twelve Oscar-nominated performances: Victor McLaglen in *The Informer* (1935), Thomas Mitchell in *The Hurricane* (1937), Mitchell in *Stagecoach* (1939), Edna May Oliver in *Drums Along the Mohawk* (1939), Jane Darwell and Henry Fonda in *The Grapes of Wrath* (1940), Sara Allgood and Donald Crisp in *How Green Was My Valley* (1941), McLaglen in *The Quiet Man* (1952), Ava Gardner and Grace Kelly in *Mogambo* (1953), and Jack Lemmon in *Mister Roberts* (1955). McLaglen won for Best Actor while Mitchell (for *Stagecoach*), Darwell, Crisp, and Lemmon won Best Supporting Oscars.

Supporting players Russell Simpson, Jane Darwell, Arthur Shields, J. Farrell MacDonald, Ward Bond, and Anna Lee, did little work of consequence away from Ford. For example, observe

Russell Simpson at the beginning of *Seven Brides for Seven Brothers* (1954) or Jane Darwell at the ball in *Gone With the Wind* (1939). Their characterizations seem flat and far less rich than their John Ford roles. Bit player Murray Alper made scores of movie appearances, usually as a wise-cracking taxi driver or bartender, but in one of his two roles for Ford, "Slug" Mahan in *They Were Expendable* (1945), his feisty sailor is unforgettable.

This was equally true with leads. Robert Montgomery and Victor Mature had long careers, but very few of their roles matched the depth of emotions they displayed in *They Were Expendable* (1945) and *My Darling Clementine* (1946), respectively. Discussing Tyrone Power's acting in *The Long Gray Line* (1955), film scholar Jeanine Basinger maintained, "Power was magnificent in a story about an ordinary man whose life added up to something special. He aged from a feisty young scrapper to a mellowed-out old man, and the true performance range that Hollywood had never allowed to blossom in Power was on full display." [8]

Why did character actors, bit players, and even stars like Maureen O'Hara and John Wayne do some of their best work for Ford? O'Hara has suggested, "He puts you at ease and sets you free to think, and you can move easily." She also recalled, "The most wonderful thing in watching Mr. Ford work was the freedom he gave his artists. He was treating everyone with artistic respect and trusted us to give every scene exactly what it needed. He never gave specific directions and I learned over time that this was the best compliment Mr. Ford could give. If John Ford gave an artist detailed directions, then you knew he thought that actor wasn't very good." Character actor Harry Carey Jr. declared, "I don't care how much he picked on me…, I was always relaxed when I worked for him. He gave me tremendous confidence, and I was never more at ease." Henry Fonda recalled that Ford hated to rehearse. "He felt that if you do a scene, particularly an emotional one, over and over again, you're going to begin to dispel or lose the original emotion." [9]

On the set, John Ford could be many things to many people. He could be an unrelenting taskmaster, especially to cast members forced upon him by a studio. He usually had little initial patience for actors of the theater, ingénues, and anyone British. If screaming, cutting sarcasm, and humiliation worked with a particular player, Ford would happily oblige. He certainly could be malicious, crude, and cruel on the set. Ava Gardner recollected her early experiences with Ford in *Mogambo* (1953): "He could be the meanest man on earth, thoroughly evil." Walter Brennan was so disgusted with John Ford's behavior on the set of *My Darling Clementine* that he told Ford he would never work for him again, and never did. [10]

At the same time, once Ford was confident in a player, he would be extremely kind, patient, and supportive, and allow that actor extensive room to work. Mary Astor worked with Ford on *The Hurricane* (1937) and observed, "I think laconic is a good word for John Ford and for his technique of direction. No big deal about communication with John. Terse, pithy, and to the point." Cinematographer Arthur C. Miller declared, "This man directs less than any man in the business. As a matter of fact, he doesn't direct–he doesn't want any actor to give an imitation of him playing the part. He wants the actor to create the part–that's why he hired him, because he saw him in the part." [11]

Ford liked to use physically unattractive character actors in his movies; *The New York Times* film critics Manohla Dargis and A.O. Scott wrote, "...he chose the lived-in faces and unmelodious voices that define his work as much as the mesas of his westerns and the towering figure of John Wayne." The big-boned bit player, bucktoothed Jack Pennick, made forty-five movies with Ford, while horse-faced Edna May Oliver, who played the widow, Mrs. McKlennan, in her one Ford film, *Drums Along the Mohawk* (1939), had the telling line, "I have a long face and I poke it where I please." [12]

Ford once declared "…it's my contention that the bits in any picture are just as important as the starring role, since they round out the story–complete the atmosphere–make the whole plausible…." Director/film scholar Lindsay Anderson contended that in *Stagecoach*, with its cast of character actors, "none of these [the characters] is profoundly drawn, but each is presented with a sharpness, an eye for the detail and interplay of personality, which gives continual color to the steadily mounting tension of the action." Tag Gallagher declared, "a Ford character may be a simpleton, or a person who never amounted to much, or someone we don't like; but he claims our attention by sensitivity and activity. Emotions are implanted into his every gesture and posture." Ford himself maintained that the secret of reaching the audience is "in people's faces, their eye expression, their movements." [13]

This naturalness, which Gallagher defined as, "the absence of an apparent distance between character and player," is there in almost all of Ford's characters, no matter how insignificant. These people are alive and genuine; they are real human beings we can relate to with their own personal foibles, fears, and warts as well as strengths and vitality. [14]

## The Book's Organization

This book contains a separate mini-chapter for each of 112 John Ford stock company members, arranged alphabetically by the actor's last name. I have chosen these particular players, each of whom participated in at least three John Ford projects, because each contributed to Ford's legacy of memorable movies and moments.

Each of these mini-chapters is comprised of the actor's photograph, the actor's date of birth (and, if apt, date of death), a listing of the actor's Ford productions, and, when possible, the actor's character names or roles in those productions. In addition, information on the actor's personal and professional life is included. To further help the reader identify the actor, this section also includes a discussion of the actor's significant non-Ford movie roles, a listing of the actor's alternative names, and a discussion of the actor's memorable Fordian characters, scenes, dialogue, and moments.

Rather than an index, this book includes two listings at the end of the book. These, together with the Table of Contents, should be helpful in cross-referencing actors and their appearances in Ford's productions. "One Hundred Twenty-Six John Ford Projects with Participating Stock Company Members" chronologically lists 117 Ford films, five documentaries, and four television episodes that feature these actors, and also includes the studios involved and a list of any of the 112 company members in the cast. "One Hundred Twelve John Ford Stock Company Members and their Ford Films, Documentaries, and Television Episodes" is a list of these 112 Ford players arranged alphabetically by last name followed by the names and dates of their John Ford productions. I have also included a listing of thirty-nine recommended readings which offer additional information on Ford's stock company.

I have attempted to be as factual as possible in listing the stock company members' films and character names, and have watched as many of John Ford's films as possible to check and recheck this data. I have consulted various sources to research lost and unavailable Ford films, but as film scholar Bill Routt has observed, many of these sources contradict one another or are incomplete. [15]

Although this book's focus is on actors, just as much a part of Ford's "family" were the cameramen, editors, writers, musicians, make-up artists, grips, production managers, composers, prop men, art directors, technicians, gaffers, set designers, and assistant directors he used repeatedly. For example, John Ford's brother, Edward O'Fearna, was Ford's assistant director in thirty-five films; while Ford's brother-in-law, Wingate Smith, was Ford's assistant director in thirty-six productions. Writers Dudley Nichols and Frank Nugent contributed to sixteen and fourteen Ford productions, respectively. Scanning the crew and production staff's credits in Ford's films, one sees the same names over and over. However, the spotlight in this book is on the players, for it is the actors and their familiar faces continually appearing in Ford's films who bring audiences the joy of recognition.

And sharing that joy of recognition is one of the basic aims of this book: realizing that Harry Tyler who played the pub owner, Pat Cohan, in *The Quiet Man* (1952) was also the outwardly tough café cook, Bert, in *The Grapes of Wrath* (1940) who sells Russell Simpson's character the bread; that Ruth Clifford who played Fleuretty Phyffe in *Wagon Master* (1950) was the schoolteacher in *Pilgrimage* (1933); that Ben Hall who played the barber in *My Darling Clementine* (1946) was Fleety Belle's brother in *Steamboat Round the Bend* (1935), and that the Bill Steele who played Nesby, the neighbor in *The Searchers* (1956) who is wounded at the battle with the Comanches by the river, is the same actor who, as Bill Gettinger, worked with Ford in at least six silent westerns in 1917!

# Endnotes

1   Roger Greenspun. "John Ford, 1895-1973." *The New York Times*, September 9, 1973, Section D, p. 15.

2   Peter Bogdanovich. *John Ford*. Berkeley: University of California Press, 1978, p. 31.

3   Scott Eyman. "John Ford in the Twenty-First Century: Why He Still Matters." In Kevin Stoehr and Michael Connolly's *John Ford in Focus: Essays on the Filmmaker's Life and Work*. Jefferson, NC: McFarland, 2008, p. 16.

4   Nevil Shute. *Vinland the Good*. New York: William Morrow, 1946, p. 125.

5   Tag Gallagher. *John Ford: The Man and His Films*. Berkeley: University of California Press, 1986, p. 482.

6   Tag Gallagher's input in his email to the author on January 21, 2012 was crucial in understanding John Ford's creation of a coherent stock company/"family unit" during his early years at Universal.

7   Howard Sharpe. "The Star Creators of Hollywood: John Ford." *Photoplay*, October 1936, p.   99.

8   Harry Carey Jr. *Company of Heroes: My Life as an Actor in the John Ford Stock Company*.   Metuchen, NJ: Scarecrow Press, 1994, p. 120.

9   Lindsay Anderson. *About John Ford*. London: Plexus, 1981, p. 217.

10 Maureen O'Hara. *'Tis Herself: A Memoir*. New York: Simon & Schuster, 2004, p. 68.

11 Dan Ford. *Pappy: The Life of John Ford*. New York: Da Capo Press, 1998, pp. 222-223.

12 Jeanine Basinger. *The Star Machine*. New York: Random House, 2007, p. 173.

13 Andrew Sinclair. *John Ford*. New York: Dial Press, 1970, p. 168.

14 Maureen O'Hara. *'Tis Herself: A Memoir*. New York: Simon & Schuster, 2004, p. 69.

15 Dan Ford. *Pappy: The Life of John Ford*. New York: De Capo Press, 1998, p. 222.

16 Lindsay Anderson. *About John Ford*. London: Plexus, 1981, p. 219.

17 Ava Gardner. *Ava: My Story*. New York: Bantam, 1990, p. 181.

18 Dan Ford. *Pappy: The Life of John Ford*. New York: De Capo Press, 1998, p. 212.

19 Mary Astor. *A Life on Film*. New York: Dell, 1972, p. 134.

20 Leonard Maltin. *The Art of the Cinematographer*. New York: Dover Press, 1978, p. 70.

21 Manohla Dargis and A.O. Scott. "The Name Might Escape, Not the Work." *The New York Times*, September 18, 2011, AR31.

22  Howard Sharpe. "The Star Creators of Hollywood: John Ford." Photoplay, October 1936, p. 99.

23  Lindsay Anderson. *About John Ford*. London: Plexus, 1981, p. 97.

24  Tag Gallagher. *John Ford: The Man and His Films*. Berkeley: University of California Press, 1986, p. 293.

25  "John Ford Taped Interviews." The John Ford Collection, Lilly Library, Indiana University, Bloomington, Indiana, tape 31, side 1, 1973.

26  Tag Gallagher. *John Ford: The Man and His Films*. Berkeley: University of California Press, 1986, p. 481.

27  Bill Routt. "Ford at Fox, Part Two (a)." *Screening the Past*. http://www.routt.net/Bill/.

# One Hundred Twelve Members of John Ford's Stock Company

### Frank Albertson

Frank Albertson (1909-1964) acted in six Ford films: *Salute* (1929) as Midshipman Albert Edward Price; *Men Without Women* (1930) as Ensign Albert Edward Price; *Born Reckless* (1930) as Frank Sheldon; *The Brat* (1931) as Stephen Forester; *Airmail* (1932) as Tommy Bogan; *The Last Hurrah* (1958) as Jack Mangan.

He was born Francis Healey Albertson in Fergus Falls, Minnesota and began his career in films as a young teenager in 1922. He worked first as a prop boy, then had a few leading roles in B-movies before spending most of his time in Hollywood as a reliable character actor, usually a smart-alecky wise guy. Over his career, he acted in over 100 motion pictures.

Frank Albertson

His most famous non-Ford role was Sam Wainwright, the former beau of Mary Hatch Bailey (Donna Reed) in *It's a Wonderful Life* (1946). Albertson's character was the guy fond of exclaiming "Hee Haw, Hee Haw!" Frank Albertson also played the hayseed playwright in the Marx Brothers' *Room Service* (1938), the wealthy rancher whose money was stolen by Janet Leigh's character in Alfred Hitchcock's *Psycho* (1960), and the mayor in *Bye Bye Birdie* (1963).

Albertson's first five Ford characters were inexperienced, open-faced youths. For example, in an early scene in *Airmail*, Albertson's young Tommy Bogan is sitting back in a chair smoking a cigarette, reading a magazine on flying, and wearing his cap backwards like his pilot heroes. Slim Summerville's older character intercedes and takes Tommy's chair, dominating the adolescent. This is a classic Fordian interchange between a callow youth and a jaded veteran, repeated scores of times in Ford's canon.

In his last Ford film, *The Last Hurrah*, Albertson portrayed a middle-aged skeptic who backs a stupid, inept politician against Spencer Tracy's incumbent. While interviewing the dim candidate and his superficial family at their home for television, Albertson's corrupt character somehow keeps a straight face amid all the exaggerated absurdity, idiocy, and din.

## Pedro Armendariz

Pedro Armendariz (1912-1963) acted in three Ford films: *The Fugitive* (1947) as the police lieutenant; *Fort Apache* (1948) as Sergeant Beaufort, and *3 Godfathers* (1948) as Pedro Roca Fuerte/ Pete.

He was born Pedro Gregorio Armendariz Hastings in Mexico and later raised in Laredo, Texas. He attended the Polytechnic Institute of San Luis Obispo in California, studying journalism and business. After graduating in 1931, he returned to Mexico and worked at various jobs until he was discovered reciting Hamlet's monologue to an American tourist by Mexican director Miguel Zacarias.

Pedro Armendariz

Pedro Armendariz became a major star in Mexico's "Golden Era of Cinema" during the mid-1940s, working with actress Dolores Del Rio and director Emilio Fernandez. At this time, Armendariz was known as "The Clark Gable of Mexico." After his three films with Ford, he continued to make motion pictures in Hollywood, Mexico, and Europe. His last role was as James Bond's (Sean Connery) Turkish espionage confederate, Kerim Bey, in *From Russia with Love* (1963).

Although Armendariz acted in only three Ford films, his roles were notable. Each of his characters was quite different from the others.

His callous, anti-religious police lieutenant in *The Fugitive* was an unforgettable brute attempting to camouflage his own secrets through violence and terror. There is a stunning scene when his character, in the midst of laughing as his men desecrate a church, abruptly halts as he hears the sound of a child's cries. It turns out that this was his own illegitimate child.

In *Fort Apache*, he portrayed an ex-Confederate officer who is now a sergeant in the U.S. cavalry:

> Sgt. Beaufort (Armendariz) is addressing a group of new recruits.

3

Beaufort: "Gentlemen, this is a horse. You will observe
it has no saddle. The reason it has no saddle is because
it'll be easier for you to stay on without the saddle.
Now, before we progress... did any of you gentlemen
have the honor of serving with the Southern arms
during the late War Between the States?"
Southern Recruit (Hank Worden): "Yes, sir. I had the
pride, sir, of serving with Bedford Forrest."
Beaufort: "I am proud to shake your hand."
Recruit: "Thank you, sir."
Beaufort: "I hope you have the pleasure of buying me
a drink on your next payday."
Recruit: "An honor, sir."
Beaufort: "You are now an acting corporal."

In *3 Godfathers*, his outlaw character displayed a wide range of emotions. During the bank robbery, when he starts to shoot his pistol, Pedro exhibits the sheer joy of the moment. Later in the desert, when he walks hat in hand to help the pregnant woman in her wagon, the gentle and religious side of his persona is revealed. After the mother dies and the trio of outlaws attempt to figure out how to bathe the baby, there is a hilarious scene when the two other inept godfathers (John Wayne and Harry Carey Jr.) take Pedro's advice and use wagon grease in place of soap or baby oil to bathe their godson.

## Frank Baker

Frank Baker (1892-1980) had small parts in twenty-seven Ford productions: *Cameo Kirby* (1923) bit; *Hearts of Oak* (1924) bit; *The Fighting Heart* (1925) manager; *Four Sons* (1928) soldier; *Hangman's House* (1928) English officer; *The Black Watch* (1929)

Highlanders officer; *Men Without Women* (1930) seaman; *Seas Beneath* (1931) bit; *Arrowsmith* (1931) ship captain; *The Lost Patrol* (1934) colonel of rescue detachment/Arab shot by sergeant; *The Informer* (1935) bit; *Steamboat Round the Bend* (1935) bit; *The Prisoner of Shark Island* (1936) bit; *Mary of Scotland* (1936) as Douglas; *The Plough and the Stars* (1936) bit; *Four Men and a Prayer* (1938) defense attorney; *Stagecoach*

Frank Baker

(1939) bit; *Drums Along the Mohawk (*1939) commander of colonel troops; *How Green Was My Valley* (1941) bit; *Fort Apache* (1948) bit; *When Willie Comes Marching Home* (1950) bit; *The Quiet Man* (1952) man in Cohan's pub; *The Bamboo Cross* episode from television's *Jane Wyman Presents* "The Fireside Theatre" series (1955) bit; *The Last Hurrah* (1958) member of Plymouth Club; *Two Rode Together* (1961) as Captain Malaprop; *The Man Who Shot Liberty Valance* (1962) poker player; *Donovan's Reef* (1963) as Captain Martin.

Baker was born in Australia and worked as an anthropologist, sailor, and filmmaker before arriving in Hollywood and working in numerous Francis Ford silent serials. John Ford met Baker through Francis, and used him in twenty-seven productions over a period of forty years. According to Baker, his refusal to kowtow to John Ford gained Ford's respect, and was the reason he was used repeatedly in Ford's movies. Frank Baker's candid interviews with film historians Tag Gallagher and Anthony Slide reveal much about Ford's company and the rivalry between the brothers John and Francis Ford.

## Chief John Big Tree

Chief John Big Tree (1877-1967) made five films with Ford: *A Fight for Love* (1919) as Swift Deer; *The Iron Horse* (1924) Cheyenne chief; *Stagecoach* (1929) Indian scout; *Drums Along the Mohawk* (1939) as Blue Back; *She Wore a Yellow Ribbon* (1949) as Apache chief, Pony That Walks.

Chief John Big Tree

John Big Tree was born Isaac John John in Buffalo, New York. According to Big Tree, he was a Seneca and was one of the three Native Americans who posed for the Indian head nickel. Big Tree also maintained that he was the model for James Earle Fraser's sculpture, "End of the Trail."

He was featured in scores of westerns from 1915 to 1950 including *The Last of the Mohicans* (1932), *Destry Rides Again* (1939), *Brigham Young* (1940), *Hudson's Bay* (1941), and *Western Union* (1941).

John Big Tree's first three roles for Ford were small. His last two roles were memorable:

One of Big Tree's most famous Ford scenes was at the beginning of *Drums Along the Mohawk* when his Blue Back's presence frightens and terrifies Claudette Colbert's young bride. At the end of the film, the victorious Americans are searching for the Tory leader, Caldwell (John Carradine). Suddenly, Big Tree's Blue Back appears from behind a pulpit and displays Caldwell's black eye patch and an immense smile.

In *She Wore a Yellow Ribbon*, Big Tree's old chief, Pony That Walks, sadly laments to John Wayne's veteran army captain, "We are too old for war" and "Too late; Nathan, too late."

## Ward Bond

Ward Bond (1903- 1960) appeared in twenty-eight Ford productions: *Salute* (1929) as football player, Midshipman Harold; *Born Reckless* (1930) sergeant; *Up the River* (1930) inmate socked by Spencer Tracy's character; *The Brat* (1931) cop; *Arrowsmith* (1931) cop; *Airmail* (1932) as doomed pilot, Joe Barnes; *Flesh* (1932) as Muscles Manning; *Submarine Patrol* (1938) as Seaman Olaf Swanson; *Young Mr. Lincoln* (1939) as John Palmer Cass; *Drums Along the Mohawk* (1939) as Adam Hartland; *The Grapes of Wrath* (1940) cop; *The Long Voyage Home* (1940) as Yank; *Tobacco Road* (1941) as Lov Bensey; *They Were Expendable* (1945) as "Boats" Mulcahey; *My Darling Clementine* (1946) as Morgan Earp; *The Fugitive* (1947) as El Gringo; *Fort Apache* (1948) as Sergeant Major Michael O'Rourke; *3 Godfathers* (1948) as Sheriff Perley "Buck" Sweet; *Wagon Master* (1950) as the Mormon leader, Elder Wiggs; the documentary, *This is Korea!* (1951) narrator; *The Quiet Man* (1952) as Father Peter Lonigan; *Rookie of the Year* episode from television's *Screen Directors Playhouse* series (1955) as

Ward Bond

Buck Goodhue, alias Buck Garrison; *The Long Gray Line* (1955) as Captain Herman J. Kohler; *Mister Roberts* (1955) as Chief

Petty Officer Dowdy; *The Searchers* (1956) as Reverend/Captain Samuel Johnston Clayton; *The Wings of Eagles* (1957) as movie director, John Dodge; the documentary, *The Growler Story* (1957) as Quincannon; *The Colter Craven Story* episode from television's *Wagon Train* series (1960) as Major Seth Adams.

Bond was born in Benkelman, Nebraska, the son of a lumberyard worker, and was raised in Denver. He grew to be a big, broad-shouldered athlete and attended USC on a football scholarship. One of his teammates was Marion Morrison, and during college, the two of them worked part-time as prop men and extras in Hollywood. Eventually, Bond became a supporting actor while Morrison became John Wayne. Bond had small parts in scores of movies including many of the classics of Hollywood's Golden Era such as the bus driver in *It Happened One Night* (1934); a Union officer in *Gone With the Wind* (1939); a cop in *The Maltese Falcon* (1942), and Burt the policeman in *It's a Wonderful Life* (1946). One of Bond's most notable non-Ford movie characters was his boxer, John L. Sullivan, in Errol Flynn's *Gentleman Jim* (1942). His most famous non-Ford role was Major Seth Adams in television's popular western series, *Wagon Train*.

On the set, the extremely right-wing Bond was often the butt of the more liberal Ford's sarcasm and practical jokes. Nevertheless, Bond's career with Ford was characterized by progressively bigger parts:

In *Young Mr. Lincoln*, Bond's bullish John Palmer Cass's air of confidence evaporates when Henry Fonda's Lincoln exposes his lies and his guilt.

In *The Long Voyage Home*, his Yank's zest for whiskey and women characterizes the lusts of his crewmates; his poignant death scene exemplifies the hollowness of such a life.

In *They Were Expendable*, his character's preamble to the enlisted men celebrating the retirement of one of their comrades (Jack Pennick) characterizes John Ford's disdain for extensive dialogue: "I'm not going to make a speech; I've just something to say."

In *Fort Apache*, there is a tender scene when Bond's Sergeant Michael O'Rourke forces himself to finish reading his scripture before embracing his son (John Agar) returning home.

In *Wagon Master*, his Elder Wiggs, leader of the Mormon wagon train, demonstrates considerable compassion and shrewdness when he uses religion and the nature of God to sway his brethren to take in a gambler and his party:

> "As I see it, He ain't one to waste His energy... an' He sure went to a lot of trouble gettin' these people into this fix. And if I was HIM, I wouldn't want anyone messin' up MY plans!"

In *The Quiet Man*, Bond's Father Lonigan has a marvelous battle with THE fish, but the highlight of the scene occurs when he bounds over a fence and joyfully witnesses the fight of fights.

Early in *The Searchers*, there is a scene when Bond's character, Reverend and Texas Ranger Captain Sam Clayton, looks away from Ethan (John Wayne) and Ethan's brother's wife (Dorothy Jordan), allowing them privacy in their secret moment of shared intimacy.

In *The Wings of Eagles*, Bond portrayed a director named John Dodge, a clone of John Ford. Bond used Ford's own pipe, dark glasses, and handkerchief, and eerily resembles the director.

## Dan Borzage

Dan Borzage (1898-1975) had small parts in sixteen Ford productions: *The Iron Horse* (1924) bit; *Stagecoach* (1939) bit; *The Long Voyage Home* (1940) as Tim; *They Were Expendable* (1945) sailor; *My Darling Clementine* (1946) accordionist; *Wagon Master* (1950) accordionist; *What Price Glory* (1952) as Gilbert; *Mister Roberts* (1955) as Jonesy; *The Searchers* (1956) accordionist at funeral; *The Wings of Eagles* (1957) as Pete; *The Last Hurrah* (1958) as Pete; *The Horse Soldiers* (1959) as Ned; *The Colton Craven Story* episode from television's *Wagon Train* series (1960) soldier; *Two Rode Together* (1961) trooper; *The Man Who Shot Liberty Valance* (1962) townsman; *Cheyenne Autumn* (1964) trooper.

Dan Borzage

Dan Borzage was born in Salt Lake City, the younger brother of director Frank Borzage, who won the first Best Director Academy Award for *7th Heaven* (1927). Dan Borzage worked with John Ford for forty years and was an important staple of the company with his accordion providing musical resonance on the set and in numerous movies such as his rendition of "Red River Valley" in *The Grapes of Wrath* and *They Were Expendable*. Borzage was with John Ford at the end; he played at Ford's funeral.

## Willis Bouchey

Willis Bouchey (1907-1977) acted in twelve John Ford productions: *Rookie of the Year* episode from television's *Screen Directors Playhouse* series (1955) as Mr. Cully; *The Long Gray Line* as Major Thomas (1955); *The Wings of Eagles* (1957) as Barton; *The Last Hurrah* (1958) as Roger Sugrue; *The Horse Soldiers* (1959) as Colonel Phil Secord; *Sergeant Rutledge* (1960) as the presiding officer at the court martial, Colonel Otis Fosgate; *The Colter Craven Story* episode from television's *Wagon Train* series (1960) as Mr. Grant; *Two Rode Together* (1961) as Mr. Harry J. Wringle; *The Man Who Shot Liberty Valance*

Willis Bouchey

(1962) as train conductor, Jason Tully; *How the West Was Won*, "*The Civil War*" *segment* (1962) surgeon; *Flashing Spikes* episode from television's *Alcoa Premier* series (1962) mayor; *Cheyenne Autumn* (1964) colonel.

Bouchey was born in Vernon, Michigan and grew up in the state of Washington. He began his film career late at the age of forty-four in a role as a doctor in the Clifton Webb comedy, *Elopement* (1951). Over the next twenty years, he appeared in almost 200 movies and television programs, often portraying ambitious men of authority, some quite pompous. He played the judge in twenty-three episodes of Raymond Burr's television series, *Perry Mason*.

Bouchey had the ability to exaggerate his characters' foibles which he did quite successfully in *The Horse Soldiers* and *Sergeant Rutledge*. Ford scholar Joseph McBride has described him as "Ford's house windbag." In *The Horse Soldiers*, Bouchey's Colonel Phil Secord, a politician-turned-army officer, is obsessed with gaining votes for the next election and has no instinct for command. Throughout the film, Secord's limitations are exposed, but never as clearly as when William Holden's medical officer declares,

"As usual, I'm just presenting the grim facts. Colonel Secord doesn't seem to understand that the coffee tastes better when the latrines are dug downstream instead of upstream. How do you like your coffee, Colonel?"

Bouchey's Colonel Otis Fosgate, the presiding officer at the court martial in *Sergeant Rutledge*, is a man characterized by impatience and exasperation, particularly when dealing with his wife (Billie Burke).

Bouchey could also deliver an ironic line of dialogue with perfect timing, as he did in *The Man Who Shot Liberty Valance* when his train conductor utters to James Stewart's senator, "Nothing's too good for the man who shot Liberty Valance."

**Frank Campeau**

Frank Campeau (1864-1943) appeared in three Ford productions: *North of Hudson Bay* (1923) as Cameron MacDonald; *Hoodman Blind* (1923) as Mark Lezzard; *3 Bad Men* (1926) as Spade Allen.

He was born in Detroit, Michigan and played skulking weasels on the stage before beginning his film career in 1911 in a Selig western one-reeler, *Kit Carson's Wooing*. He acted in over ninety movies between 1911 and 1940. His role as a reformed bandit in *Jordan is a Hard Road* (1915) starring Dorothy Gish had some similarities to his most famous Ford role in *3 Bad Men*. He played the villain in numerous silent and early sound westerns, and also was the shifty-eyed antagonist in several Douglas Fairbanks silents, such as *His Majesty the American* (1919), *Till the Clouds Roll By* (1919), and *The Nut* (1921), in which he played a character impersonating General Ulysses S. Grant. (In 1930, he was General Philip Sheridan in D.W. Griffith's *Abraham Lincoln*).

Frank Campeau

Campeau played a despicable murderer in Ford's *North of Hudson Bay* and a crooked lawyer in Ford's *Hoodman Blind*; both appear to be contemptible scoundrels who bring on the hisses. But it is Campeau's Spade Allen in John Ford's second silent western epic, *3 Bad Men*, that is his most memorable role. Allen is an immoral card shark and murderer who is one of three outlaws (along with J. Farrell MacDonald's Mike Costigan and Tom Santschi's Bull Stanley) who befriend the film's hero, Dan O'Malley (George O'Brien), so they can marry him off to their ward (Olive Borden). With his tall stove pipe hat and his perpetual scowl, Frank Campeau does an impressive job portraying an extremely intriguing "good badman" who, along with his two partners, eventually sacrifices his life for the young lovers.

## Harry Carey

Harry Carey (1878-1947) appeared in twenty-six Ford productions: *The Soul Herder* (1917) as Cheyenne Harry; *Cheyenne's Pal* (1917) as Cheyenne Harry; *Straight Shooting* (1917) as Cheyenne Harry; *The Secret Man* (1917) as Cheyenne Harry; *A Marked Man* (1917) as Cheyenne Harry; *Bucking Broadway* (1917) as Cheyenne Harry; *The Phantom Riders* (1918) as Cheyenne Harry; *Wild Women* (1918) as Cheyenne Harry; *Thieves' Gold* (1918) as Cheyenne Harry; *The Scarlet Drop* (1918) as "Kaintuck" Harry Ridge; *Hell Bent* (1918) as Cheyenne Harry; *A Woman's Fool* (1918) as Lin McLean; *Three Mounted Men* (1918)

13

Harry Carey

as Cheyenne Harry; *Roped* (1919) as Cheyenne Harry; *A Fight for Love* (1919) as Cheyenne Harry; *Bare Fists* (1919) as Cheyenne Harry; *Riders of Vengeance* (1919) as Cheyenne Harry; *Outcasts of Poker Flat* (1919) as Square Shootin' Harry Lanyon/John Oakhurst; *The Ace of the Saddle* (1919) as Cheyenne Harry Henderson; *The Rider of the Law* (1919) as Jim Kyneton; *A Gun Fightin' Gentleman* (1919) as Cheyenne Harry; *Marked Men* (1919) as Cheyenne Harry; *The Freeze-Out* (1921) as the stranger, Ohio; *The Wallop* (1921) as John Wesley Pringle; *Desperate Trails* (1921) as Bart Carson; *The Prisoner of Shark Island* (1936) commandant of Fort Jefferson.

Harry Carey was born in New York City, the son of a judge. He attended New York University intending to become a lawyer, but a boating accident and the resulting pneumonia forced him to leave school. He began writing plays and acting in them, and eventually worked with D.W. Griffith in the Biograph Company in 1912. He followed Griffith to Hollywood and soon became a successful silent film star. He joined Universal in 1915 and within two years developed a close professional relationship and friendship with the young director, John Ford. After his numerous Universal westerns with Ford, he made scores of silent, early sound, and serial westerns before becoming a character actor during the late 1930s and 1940s. Four of his noteworthy non-Ford roles were the title role in *Trader Horn* (1931), Hawkeye in *Last of the Mohicans* (1932), the gum-chewing president of the Senate in *Mr. Smith Goes to Washington* (1939) for which he earned an Academy

Award nomination for Best Supporting Actor, and the persistent sheriff, Wistful McClintock, in John Wayne's *Angel and the Bad Man* (1947).

John Ford's biggest early influence in Hollywood—after his brother, Francis—was Harry Carey who helped mentor Ford at the beginning of the young director's career. The two men collaborated on all aspects of filming their silent westerns including establishing a comfortable company of players that helped create a positive working milieu. Carey and Ford stopped working together in 1921 and made only one more picture together, *The Prisoner of Shark Island*, in 1936. Ford's jealousy of Carey's salary and Harry Carey's acceptance of negative gossip about Ford contributed to the break-up. At the beginning of *3 Godfathers*, a film that prominently featured Carey's son, Harry Carey Jr., there is a dedication to the recently deceased Carey: "To the memory of Harry Carey–bright star of the early western sky."

In all of his silent westerns with Ford, Carey played a "good badman;" in a majority of them, he played the character "Cheyenne Harry." In Ford's first feature, *Straight Shooting*, one of the only surviving early John Ford films, there are numerous scenes that display Carey's most famous character:

In the scene that introduces Cheyenne Harry, a lawman nails a wanted poster onto a large tree, offering a $1000 reward for the capture of Harry. Once the sheriff leaves, a smirking Harry appears from within a hole behind a branch and sneers at the poster.

In the pivotal and emotional scene when Harry watches the farmer he has been hired to kill mourn for his dead son, the brim of Harry's hat symbolically causes a shadow that covers his eyes until he takes it off. Soon, he vows to side with the nesters.

After the showdown with Fremont, Cheyenne Harry's distress over killing a former drinking buddy is expressed when Cheyenne walks to his horse and sadly grasps the horse's tail.

At the end of the movie when Harry wavers between staying with Joan (Molly Malone) and leaving, he sits alone on a rock and holds his elbow in his signature Harry Carey gesture that John Wayne would use almost forty years later in *The Searchers*.

## Harry Carey Jr.

Harry Carey Jr. (1921—2012) acted in ten Ford productions: *3 Godfathers* (1948) as William Kearney/The Abilene Kid; *She Wore a Yellow Ribbon* (1949) as 2nd Lt. Ross Pennell; *Wagon Master* (1950) as Sandy Owens; *Rio Grande* (1950) as Trooper Daniel "Sandy" Boone; *The Long Gray Line* (1955) as the plebe, Whitey, (Dwight D. Eisenhower); *Mister Roberts* (1955) as Stefanowski; *The Searchers* (1956) as Brad Jorgensen; *Two Rode Together* (1961) as Ortho Clegg; *Flashing Spikes* episode from television's *Alcoa Premier* series (1962) man in dugout; *Cheyenne Autumn* (1964) as Trooper Smith.

Carey was born in Saugus, California, the son of Harry and Olive Carey, both significant members of John Ford's stock company. His nickname of Dobe was based on his red hair, the color of adobe bricks. During his long fifty-year career, Carey Jr. appeared in almost 200 movies and television episodes, usually in westerns. His non-Ford film credits include *Red River* (1948), *Mask* (1985), *The Whales of August* (1987), and *Tombstone* (1993). His most famous television role was the cowboy, Bill Burnett, in the Walt Disney television series, *Spin and Marty* (1955-57). His wife Marilyn is the daughter of character actor, Paul Fix.

One of Carey Jr.'s biggest contributions to the Ford troupe was his 1994 book, *Company of Heroes: My Life as an Actor in The John Ford Stock Company*, in which he vividly describes working for Ford.

His most remembered Fordian characters were usually baby-faced youths. In *3 Godfathers,* his "Abilene Kid" is a boy desperately trying to be a man and gain the respect of his two partners. In the desert, the Kid sings a beautiful rendition of "The Streets of Laredo."

He had two solid scenes in *She Wore a Yellow Ribbon.* One is when his young 2nd Lt. Pennell attempts to go "picnic-ing" with Olivia

Harry Carey Jr.

(Joanne Dru). The other is when he, Sgt. Tyree (Ben Johnson), and Captain Brittles (John Wayne) watch from a distance as Apaches torture gunrunners who attempted to cheat them:

> Captain Brittles to Sgt. Tyree: "Join me in a chaw of tobacco?"
> Sgt. Tyree: "No, sir. I don't chaw and I don't play cards."
> Captain Brittles: "Chawing tobacco is a nasty habit. Been known to turn a man's stomach."
> 2nd Lt. Ross Pennell: "I'll take a chaw if you please, sir."

*Wagon Master* starred supporting actors Ben Johnson, Ward Bond, and Carey Jr. There is great comical rapport between the three actors throughout the movie. Dobe also has some amusing dialogue with his Mormon rival, Jackson (Don Summers), for the attention of Prudence (Kathleen O'Malley):

Sandy: "Be hotter 'n hell by noon."

Jackson: "Mind your language!"

Sandy: "I wasn't cussin'"

Jackson: "Said 'hell'."

Sandy: "'Hell' ain't cussin'... It's... it's geography... a name of a place, like you might say Abilene or Salt Lake City..."

Jackson: "Don't you go makin' any remarks about Salt Lake City!"

In *Rio Grande*, Carey Jr.'s young soldier has several memorable scenes such as giving guff to his sergeant (Victor McLaglen); announcing his name, Daniel Boone, to a marshal (Grant Withers) searching for a fugitive from Texas, and, of course, riding "Roman-style" alongside his partner, Ben Johnson.

## Olive Carey

Olive Carey (1896-1988) acted in three Ford films: *The Searchers* (1956) as Mrs. Jorgensen; *The Wings of Eagles* (1957) as Brisy O'Faolain; *Two Rode Together* (1961) as Abby Frazer.

Olive Carey

She was born Olive Fuller Golden in New York City. From a young age, she was interested in acting; her father was prominent in theatrical unionization. When she was eighteen she appeared in her first silent film, *Tess of the Storm Country* (1914). She gave up her career after she married Harry Carey in 1916. She made a few films in the 1930s, including *Trader Horn* with her husband in 1931, but focused on raising her two children; one was character actor, Harry Carey Jr., who later joined Ford's company. After her husband's death in 1947, she resumed her acting career, appearing in motion pictures and, later, numerous television episodes. Perhaps her most memorable non-Ford role was Ma Clanton in *Gunfight at the O.K. Corral* (1955) starring Burt Lancaster and Kirk Douglas.

Olive Carey was a serious looking woman in her sixties when she worked on Ford's three films. Her most memorable role was Mrs. Jorgenson in *The Searchers*, a tough, self-sufficient woman who demonstrates an enormous amount of emotional strength:

> Lars Jorgensen (John Qualen): "It's this country killed my boy. Yes, by golly, I tell you..." Mrs. Jorgensen: "No, Lars. It just so happens we be Texicans. Texican is nothing but a human man way out on a limb. This year and next, and maybe for a hundred more. But I don't think it'll be forever. Someday this country's gonna be a fine, good place to be. Maybe it needs our bones in the ground before that time can come."

## John Carradine

John Carradine (1906-1988) appeared in twelve Ford productions: *The Prisoner of Shark Island* (1936) as Sgt. Rankin; *Mary of Scotland* (1936) as Rizzio; *The Hurricane* (1936) warden; *Four Men and a Prayer* (1938) as Gen. Adolfo Arturo Sebastian; *Submarine Patrol* (1938) as McAllison; *Stagecoach* (1939) as the gambler, Hatfield; *Drums Along the Mohawk* (1939) as the Tory leader, Caldwell; *The Grapes of Wrath* (1940) as Casey; *The Last Hurrah* (1958) as the political leader, Amos Force; *The Colter Craven*

John Carradine

*Story* episode from television's *Wagon Train* series (1960) as Park Cleatus; *The Man Who Shot Liberty Valance* (1962) as outspoken politician, Maj. Cassius Starbuckle; *Cheyenne Autumn* (1964) as gambler, Jeff Blair.

He was born Richmond Reed Carradine in New York City and raised in Poughkeepsie in upstate New York. He originally wanted to be a painter and sculptor but his strong, distinctive voice and his commanding presence made him a natural for the new sound films, and by 1932 he was in Hollywood acting in *Tol'able David* under the name John Peter Richmond. Soon, he became one of the busiest actors in the business, leaving him little time to devote to his beloved Shakespearian productions.

In his non-Ford career, Carradine played the villain in countless movies but he also occasionally portrayed sympathetic characters. Although most of his latter performances were in B or worse movies, he will be remembered for his powerful voice; his acting sons, David, Keith, and Robert, and his roles in Ford films. Five notable non-Ford roles were: his Bartolomeo Romagna in *Winterset* (1936); his Bob Ford, the dirty little coward who shot "Mr. Howard," in *Jesse James* (1939); his poignant dying prisoner, Coughy, in *Captain Fury* (1939); his zealous Mormon scout Porter Rockwell in *Brigham Young–Frontiersman* (1940), and his lively Bret Harte in *The Adventures of Mark Twain* (1944).

Although his villains in *The Prisoner of Shark Island, The Hurricane,* and *Drums Along the Mohawk* are singular characters, his legacy in Ford's films revolves around the gambler Hatfield in *Stagecoach* and the defrocked preacher Casey in *The Grapes of Wrath*.

Hatfield is a tragic casualty of the American Civil War whose stubborn refusal to bend with the times dooms him. Utilizing his voice, sly mannerisms, and subtle gestures, Carradine captures the gambler's inconsistencies; Hatfield is a gallant and genteel man who has been rumored to have shot opponents in the back. He demonstrates his chivalry in the scene in the stagecoach during the Indian attack when he gives Mrs. Mallory (Louise Plat) his derringer.

In an earlier scene filled with nostalgia and the soft tune of "I Dream of Jeannie with the Light Brown Hair" in the background, Lucy Mallory and Hatfield recall the Old South, exchanging thoughts about their shared Southern heritage:

> Lucy: "You've been very kind. Why?"
> Hatfield: "The world I live in, one doesn't often meet a lady, Mrs. Mallory."
> Lucy: "Have you ever been in Virginia?"
> Hatfield: "I was in your father's regiment."
> Lucy: "I should remember your name. You're Mr. Hatfield."
> Hatfield: "That's what I'm called, yes."

In *The Grapes of Wrath*, in the role of his life, John Carradine played Jim Casey, a former preacher who has lost his religious calling. Jim Casey is the moral voice of the movie and slowly evolves into an advocate and spokesman for the unity of all mankind. His martyrdom results in Tom Joad's transformation into a social activist. Casey has several great lines, including:

"Tom, you gotta learn like I'm learnin'. I don't know it right yet myself. That's why I can't ever be a preacher again. Preachers gotta know. I don't know. I gotta ask."

## Spencer Charters

Spencer Charters (1875-1943) appeared in four Ford productions: *The Hurricane* (1936) judge; *Young Mr. Lincoln* (1939) as Judge Herbert A. Bell; *Drums Along the Mohawk* (1939) as the innkeeper, Mr. J. Fisk; *Tobacco Road* (1941) county clerk.

Charters was born in Duncannon, Pennsylvania and after many years on stage, he began his film career when he was forty-five in a Marion Davies silent, *April Folly* (1920). He was a short, stout fellow with a great smile and chuckle. Charters had small parts in over 220 movies, often playing inquisitive little men. His final role was a brief bit as the hard-of-hearing marriage license clerk, early in Cary Grant's *Arsenic and Old Lace* (1944).

Although he only made four films with Ford, his small but distinctive parts in *Young Mr. Lincoln* and *Drums Along the Mohawk* are notable.

Presiding over the murder trial in *Young Mr. Lincoln*, Charters' Judge Herbert A. Bell listens to a young Abe Lincoln (Henry Fonda) cross-examining a hostile witness, J. Palmer Cass (Ward Bond), and asking him about his name:

Lincoln: "Why 'J. Palmer Cass?' Why not 'John P. Cass'?"
Cass: "Well, I..."
Lincoln: "Does 'J. Palmer Cass' have something to hide?"
Cass: "No."

Lincoln: "Then what do you part your name in the middle for?"
Cass: "I got a right to call myself anything I want as long as it's my own name!"
Lincoln: "Well then if it's all the same to you, I'll call you Jack Cass."
There's a roar of laughter from the spectators until the judge's gavel silences them.

Spencer Charters

Then, suddenly, a few minutes later, the judge cackles with mirth, "Jack-ass. I just got it!" He laughs hysterically.

At the beginning of *Drums Along the Mohawk*, Gil Martin (Henry Fonda) and his bride Lara (Claudette Colbert) are staying at the Kings Road Tavern on their wedding night. Charter's half-deaf innkeeper, Mr. Fisk, serves them dinner holding the longest pipe in the world.

Fisk: "Been married long?"
Gil: "No, not so long."
Fisk: "How long?"
Gil: "Not so long!"
Fisk chuckles.
Fisk: "I thought that's what you said." More chuckles. "I knew it the minute I laid eyes on you. Honeymooners!" Lots of laughter. "You got it written all over both of you." More laughter.

A few minutes later, after a stranger (John Carradine) with a black patch over one eye approaches them and asks a lot of questions, the innkeeper reappears.

> Fisk: "That's a queer one, ain't he? Too many questions to suit me. With that patch over his eye, I bet he lost it trying to see something that wasn't any of his business."

## Berton Churchill

Berton Churchill (1876-1940) appeared in five Ford productions: *Doctor Bull* (1933) as Herbert Banning; *Judge Priest* (1934) as Senator Horace Maydew; *Steamboat Round the Bend* (1935) as "The New Moses"; *Four Men and a Prayer* (1938) as Mr. Martin Cherrington; *Stagecoach* (1939) as the banker, Gatewood.

Berton Churchill

Churchill was a Canadian born in Toronto who began his career as a theatrical actor. He had an intimidating, commanding presence and the perfect affected voice for villains and pompous politicians. While on Broadway, he was one of the first members of Actors Equity. In the late 1920s, with the advent of sound, he moved to Hollywood and appeared in over 100 productions during the 1930s. He helped start the Manners Club in 1925 which eventually led to his involvement in creating the Screen Actors Guild in 1933. Radio star Harold Peary claimed he based much of his famous character, "The Great Gildersleeve," on the haughty pretensions of Churchill's film characterizations.

Churchill will always be remembered for his supercilious banker Gatewood in *Stagecoach*. However, he could also do comedy, as demonstrated by his "The New Moses" preacher character in *Steamboat Round the Bend* whose every exaggerated word and gesture is amusing.

In *Stagecoach*, his self-righteous banker stands on his soapbox while sitting in the coach, and lectures his fellow passengers about banks and government as he clasps onto his valise filled with embezzled funds:

> "I don't know what the government is coming to. Instead of protecting businessmen,
>
> it pokes its nose into business! Why, they're even talking now about having bank examiners. As if we bankers don't know how to run our own banks! Why, at home I have a letter from a popinjay official saying they were going to inspect my books.... The government must not interfere with business!... What this country needs is a businessman for president!"

## Ruth Clifford

Ruth Clifford (1900-1998) appeared in eleven Ford productions: *The Face on the Bar-Room Floor* (1923) as Marion Trevor; *Pilgrimage* (1933) schoolteacher; *Four Men and a Prayer* (1938) telephone operator; *Drums Along the Mohawk* (1939) woman wearing military coat at the end of the movie when the fort is under attack by Indians and Tories; *How Green Was My Valley* (1941) village woman gossiper; *3 Godfathers* (1948) woman in bar when John Wayne's character carries in the baby; *Wagon Master* (1950) as Fleuretty Phyffe; *The Quiet Man* (1952) mother;

*The Searchers* (1956) deranged woman at fort; *The Last Hurrah* (1958) nurse; *Two Rode Together* (1961) bit.

Clifford was born in Pawtucket, Rhode Island but after the death of her mother in 1911, she moved to Los Angeles to live with her actress aunt. As a teenager, she began acting in silent films and

by her mid-twenties she was playing leads in several important films, including the part of Ann Rutledge in *The Dramatic Life of Abraham Lincoln* (1924). With the advent of sound in the late 1920s, her roles became less significant. For a time, she was married to James Cornelius, a prosperous Beverly Hills real estate developer.

Clifford was one of John Ford's favorite bridge partners. She told film scholar Anthony Slide that Ford

Ruth Clifford

hired certain players such as herself so they would go on location and play bridge with him, one of his favorite evening recreations.

The majority of Ruth Clifford's parts in Ford films were quite small, but she had an important role in *Wagon Master* as Fleuretty Phyffe, actor Locksley Hall's (Alan Mowbray) fiancée of twelve years. She is the force that pushes Hall onward and is a mentor for her younger fellow performer, Denver (Joanne Dru).

## Donald Crisp

Donald Crisp (1882-1974) participated in five Ford productions: *Mary of Scotland* (1936) as Huntley; *How Green Was My Valley* (1941) as Mr. Morgan; the documentary, *The Battle of Midway* (1942) narrator; *The Long Gray Line* (1955) as Old

Martin; *The Last Hurrah* (1958) as Cardinal Martin Burke. He won the Best Supporting Actor Academy Award for his work in *How Green Was My Valley.*

Crisp was born in Scotland and fought in the Boer War in South Africa. He migrated to the United States in 1906 and worked as a stage actor and opera singer until 1910 when he joined director D.W. Griffith in Hollywood. He worked with Griffith as an actor and as an assistant director. He directed some of the battle scenes in *Birth of a Nation* (1915) and played General

Donald Crisp

Grant. His most famous role for Griffith was the prizefighting brute, Battling Burrows, who beats his daughter (Lillian Gish) to death in *Broken Blossoms* (1919).

Between 1916 and 1930, Crisp directed forty-six films including *The Navigator* (1924) starring his co-director, Buster Keaton, and *Don Q, Son of Zorro* (1925) starring Douglas Fairbanks. After 1930, he devoted himself to acting and to banking; he was quite successful financially, and was a member of the advisory board to the Bank of America concerning loans to the studios. He had numerous noteworthy non-Ford roles during Hollywood's Golden Era such as his fathers in *Lassie Come Home* (1943) and *National Velvet* (1944); his senior officers in *The Charge of the Light Brigade* (1936) and *The Dawn Patrol* (1938), and his doctors in *Jezebel* (1938) and *Wuthering Heights* (1939).

Crisp's characters for Ford were quite diverse. In *Mary of Scotland*, he was a Scottish laird loyal to Queen Mary (Katharine Hepburn); in *How Green Was My Valley*, he was a Welsh miner; in

*The Long Gray Line*, he was a chatty Irishman; in *The Last Hurrah*, he was an American cardinal. All were memorable men, but it was the Welshman, Gwilym Morgan, classic Hollywood's definitive father, who was Crisp's greatest accomplishment. Morgan is warm yet stern, courageous yet shortsighted, easy to anger yet exceedingly sentimental.

*How Green Was My Valley* is filled with treasured Fordian moments involving Crisp's character. There are the early scenes with Crisp's father pointing out the world to his young son, Huw (Roddy McDowall). There is the scene at the dinner table when Huw grabs a piece of bread before his father does, and is reprimanded by an angry scowl. There are the comic moments when Mrs. Morgan (Sara Allgood) puts her husband in his place. And there is the poignant scene at the dinner table when after all of his brothers have angrily departed, Huw taps his plate with his knife and fork until Gwilym Morgan lovingly declares, "Yes, my son, I know you are there."

## Ken Curtis

Ken Curtis (1916-1991) appeared in thirteen Ford productions: *Rio Grande* (1950) as regimental singer, Donnelly; *The Quiet Man* (1952) as Dermot Fahy; *The Long Gray Line* (1955) bit; *Mister Roberts* (1955) as Yeoman 3rd Class Dolan; *The Searchers* (1956) as Charlie McCorry; *The Wings of Eagles* (1957) as John Dale Price; the documentary, *The Growler Story* (1957) as Captain Howard W. Gilmore; *The Last Hurrah* (1958) as Monsignor Killian; *The Horse Soldiers* (1959) as the Union scout, Wilkie; *The Colter Craven Story* episode from television's *Wagon Train* series (1960) as Kyle Cleatus; *Two Rode Together* (1961) as Greeley Clegg; *How the West Was Won*, "*The Civil War*" segment (1962) bit; *Cheyenne Autumn* (1964) as Joe.

Curtis was born Curtis Wain Gates in southeastern Colorado, the son of a town sheriff. He was originally a singer and sang with Tommy Dorsey and the Sons of the Pioneers. He starred in several musical B-westerns in the late 1940s before appearing in John Ford's *Rio Grande*. He was married to Ford's daughter Barbara from 1952 to 1964.

Ken Curtis

He played Captain Almeron Dickinson in John Wayne's *The Alamo* (1960); co-starred with Larry Pennell in the skydiving television series *Ripcord* (1961-1963), and was the voice of the vulture, Nutsy, in Disney's animated version of *Robin Hood* (1973). He is best known for his character Festus, the illiterate prison custodian in television's *Gunsmoke*. His last role was the old rancher, Seaborn Tay, in the Louis L'Amour television western, *Conagher* (1991), starring Sam Elliott and Katharine Ross.

Ken Curtis' Fordian characters were each fair-minded, spirited men, unafraid to fight the good fight. In *The Quiet Man*, Dermot Fahy has no difficulty standing up to the Squire (Victor McLaglen); in *The Searchers*, Charlie McCorry is willing to fight Marty (Jeffrey Hunter) for Laurie (Vera Miles) ("I'll thank you to unhand my fi-an-cy"); in *The Last Hurrah*, his Monsignor Killian has no problem playing golf with a rabbi.

The scene and dialogue from *The Quiet Man* in Cohan's crowded pub is particularly noteworthy. A frustrated Squire Danaher, outbid by Sean Thornton (John Wayne) for the cottage, publicly criticizes Sean for overspending:

Danaher loudly declares, "And I bid no welcome to any man fool enough to pay a thousand pounds for a bit of land that isn't worth two hundred."

Fahy interjects, "Didn't I hear of someone named Danaher bidding to eight hundred and ten?"

Danaher angrily calls to his man, "Get your book out. Put his name down. Dermot Fahy."

A spirited Fahy replies, "F-A-H-Y. No E's, Squireen Danaher."

### Jane Darwell

Jane Darwell (1879-1967) participated in seven Ford productions: *The Grapes of Wrath* (1940) as Ma Joad; the documentary, *The Battle of Midway* (1942) narrator; *My Darling Clementine* (1946) as Kate Nelson; *3 Godfathers* (1948) as Miss Florie; *Wagon Master* (1950) as Sister Ledeyard; *The Sun Shines Bright* (1953) as Mrs. Aurora Ratchitt; *The Last Hurrah* (1958) as Delia Boylan.

Jane Darwell was born Patty Mary Woodward in Palmyra, Missouri, the daughter of a railroad president who claimed to be a direct descendant of President Andrew Jackson. Originally, she wanted to be a circus performer or an opera singer, but eventually focused on the stage. She made her first movie in 1913, but she was not successful until the advent of sound. From that point on, she kept busy portraying strong-willed yet kindly housekeepers, mothers, and grandmothers. She

Jane Darwell

occasionally played villainous characters, like her shrew in *The Oxbow Incident* (1943), egging on the lynch mob. Her last movie appearance was the Bird Woman in *Mary Poppins* (1964). One of her favorite quotes was, "I've played Henry Fonda's mother so often that, whenever we run into each other, I call him 'Son' and he calls me 'Ma' just to save time."

Darwell played both serious and comic roles; this was demonstrated in her work with Ford. Her man-crazy Miss Florie in *3 Godfathers* and her trumpet-blasting Sister Ledeyard in *Wagon Master* are comical characters who added humor to serious storylines. And then there is her Ma Joad. Darwell's performance as a woman who balances fearful vulnerability with significant strength of character was the apex of her career highlighted by this dialogue:

> "Well, Pa, a woman can change better'n a man. A man lives sorta–well, in jerks. Baby's born or somebody dies, and that's a jerk. He gets a farm or loses it, and that's a jerk. With a woman, it's all in one flow, like a stream–little eddies and waterfalls–but the river, it goes right on. Woman looks at it thata way."
>
> "Rich fellas come up an' they die, an' their kids ain't no good an' they die out. But we keep a' comin. We're the people that live. They can't wipe us out; they can't lick us. We'll go on forever, Pa, 'cause we're the people."

## Andy Devine

Andy Devine (1905-1977) appeared in five Ford productions: *Doctor Bull* (1933) as soda jerk, Larry Ward; *Stagecoach* (1939) as Buck; *Two Rode Together* (1961) as Sgt. Darius P. Posey; *The Man*

*Who Shot Liberty Valance* (1962) as Marshal Link Appleyard; *How the West Was Won*, *"The Civil War" segment* (1962) as Cpl. Peterson.

Devine was born in Flagstaff, Arizona and was an excellent athlete as a youth. He played football for several colleges including

Santa Clara University, and this experience helped bolster his career as many of his early films focused on football. His croaking, raspy, high-pitched voice soon became his trademark and by the mid-1930s he had established himself as a plump, silly sidekick or a country bumpkin offering comic relief. Devine made over 150 movies and television episodes from 1928 through 1977. His two most famous roles were television's Wild Bill Hickok's (Guy Madison) partner, Jingles B. Jones, and the host of the children's

Andy Devine

television show, *Andy's Gang*.

Andy Devine's five Ford characters added humor, cheer, and balance to the serious sides of the storylines. For example, his soda jerk hypochondriac in *Doctor Bull*; his stagecoach driver, Buck, in *Stagecoach*, and his cowardly Marshal Link Appleyard in *The Man Who Shot Liberty Valance* each in their own way took the edge off their films' dramatic tension.

In *Stagecoach*, Mrs. Mallory (Louise Platt) has just given birth. Buck calls out to the Marshal, Curly (George Bancroft), "Hey, Curly, do you think I oughta charge Mrs. Mallory's baby half fare?"

Later, Buck and the Marshal discuss the impending fight between Ringo (John Wayne) and Luke Plummer (Tom Tyler):

Buck: "If I was you, I'd let them shoot it out."
Marshal Curly Wilcox: "Let who?"
Buck: "Luke Plummer and the Kid. There would be a lot more peace in this territory if that Luke Plummer had so many holes in him he couldn't hold his liquor."

Just one glance at Devine's timid peace officer, Link Appleyard, in *The Man Who Shot Liberty Valance*, and the audience knows they are seeing a very frightened man:

Appleyard: "As long as he (Lee Marvin's Liberty Valance) behaves himself in this town, I ain't got no, ah..."
Ransom Stoddard (Jimmy Stewart): "...Jurisdiction."
Link Appleyard: "What he said is right. I ain't got none of it."

## James Donlan

James Donlan (1888-1938) was in four Ford productions: *Airmail* (1932) airplane passenger passing out cigars; *Pilgrimage* (1933) barber; *Doctor Bull* (1933) as Bull's supporter, Harry Weems; *The Whole Town's Talking* (1935) as policeman, Detective Sgt. Howe.

He was born in San Francisco and worked as a singer and an actor in a variety of venues as a young man. He had parts in two short-lived Broadway plays, *Home Again* (1918) and *The Lady Killer* (1924), before moving to Hollywood in 1929. For the next decade, he acted in over 100 films, usually playing Irishmen in small roles. One of his larger parts was the boxing manager, Kirby, in Mae West's *Belle of the Nineties* (1934). Donlan's daughter, actress Yolande Donlan, wrote a 1976 autobiography, *Shake the*

*Stars Down*, in which she described her father's busy life and schedule during the 1930s.

Donlan's roles for John Ford were small, but notable. His jovial airline passenger happily passing out cigars after landing in bad weather in *Airmail* dominates a brief scene (even though one of the great scene-stealers, Francis Ford, plays another passenger in the throng). And in *The Whole Town's Talking*, Donlan's cocky,

James Donlan

bumbling, gum-chewing police sergeant adds to the wackiness of the mistaken identity scenario.

## Mimi Doyle

Mimi Doyle (1913?-1979) appeared in seven Ford productions: *Four Men and a Prayer* (1938) Buenos Aires telephone operator; *When Willie Comes Marching Home* (1950) girl at party; *The Quiet Man* (1952) Dan Tobin's (Francis Ford) daughter in the interior shot by his bed; *The Sun Shines Bright* (1953) bit; *The Long Gray Line* (1955) nun; *Mister Roberts* (1955) nurse; *The Last Hurrah* (1958) as Mamie Burns.

It appears she was born in Los Angeles, the sister of Patricia Doyle who was married to film director Robert Wise (*West Side Story* [1961] and *The Sound of Music* [1965]) from 1942 to her death in 1975. Apparently, Mimi and her sister, Patricia, worked as stand-ins for several movie stars including Irene Dunne and Katharine Hepburn, and were friends of Miss Hepburn. Mimi Doyle's first credit is the Hepburn costume melodrama, *Quality Street* (1937), in which Mimi Dole is listed as a stand-in. Between

1938 and 1976, Doyle made appearances in over thirty movies and television episodes. The majority of these were uncredited bit roles. Aka Mimi Dole, Mimi Doyle, Murph Doyle Root.

None of Mimi Doyle's roles in Ford's films were particularly noteworthy. In *The Quiet Man*, she played Dan Tobin's (Francis Ford) daughter by his bedside, filmed in the studio; another actress (Maureen Coyne) played the daughter in exterior scenes filmed in Ireland.

Interest in Mimi Doyle was provoked by a passage in Maureen O'Hara's 2004 autobiography:

> "I wonder if John Ford was struggling with conflicts within himself. These conflicts were manifested as anger towards me, his friends, his family, his heroes, and most of all, himself. His fantasies and crushes on women like me, Kate Hepburn, Anna Lee, and Murph Doyle—all of whom he professed love for at one time or another —were just balm for this wound."

There is a revealing correspondence to John Ford (in the Ford Papers at Indiana University's Lilly Library and reprinted, in part, in Scott Eyman's *Print the Legend*), that ends with "Good night my darling," and signed "Mimi." The letter recounts a supposed conversation between "Miss D" and Katharine Hepburn in which Hepburn talks of her relationship with Ford at the time of *Mary of*

Mimi Doyle

*Scotland* (1936) and reasons why the relationship failed. The letter contains several observations about Ford including, "Had he been happy–he never would have been the artist that he is today." The letter concludes with Mimi's repeated declarations of her love for "My Darling."

## Stepin Fetchit

Stepin Fetchit (1902?-1985) was in five Ford productions: *Salute* (1929) as Smoke Screen; *The World Moves On* (1934) as

Stepin Fetchit

Dixie; *Judge Priest* (1934) as Jeff Poindexter; *Steamboat Round the Bend* (1934) as Jonah; *The Sun Shines Bright* (1953) as Jeff Poindexter.

He was born Lincoln Theodore Monroe Andrew Perry between 1892 and 1902 to West Indian parents in Key West, Florida. As a young man, he created the character "The Laziest Man in the World" that he would develop throughout his career. Fetchit always claimed that he got his stage name from a race horse, but it is more likely that "Step 'n Fetchit" was the name of a partnership he was originally in, and after he went solo, he continued to use the name. Aka Step'n Fetchit, Strepin' Fetchit.

After years of performing in medicine shows and vaudeville, he arrived in Hollywood in the late 1920s and debuted in *In Old Kentucky* (1927). All of his roles, both in and out of Ford films, featured lethargic, sluggish, easily frightened comical African American characters who were continually mumbling. Contemporary African Americans were proud of his financial success and his subtle taunting of "The Man," but they (and white audiences) increasingly grew uncomfortable with his characters' "Uncle Tomism," and by the mid-1940s, he was bankrupt and couldn't find work. Ford attempted to get Fetchit a part in *My Darling Clementine* but the studio refused; it wasn't until 1952 in *The Sun Shines Bright* that Fetchit and Ford did another movie together. Late in life, he began making a few films, was honored by various African American organizations, and developed a friendship with boxer Cassius Clay; both converted to Islam.

Each of Fetchit's characters in John Ford's pictures were examples of Ford's wise rustic fools. For example, there is a brief scene in *Steamboat Round the Bend* when "The New Moses" (Berton Churchill) is pulled out of the river and Fetchit's wide-eyed Jonah offers him a glass of water. This scene hints that Jonah is not quite the idiot everyone thinks he is, but rather a man who is very shrewdly putting down his alleged betters.

## Shug Fisher

Shug Fisher (1907-1984) appeared in five Ford productions: *Rio Grande* (1950) regimental singer/bugler; *Mister Roberts* (1955) as Johnson; *Sergeant Rutledge* (1960) as Mr. Owens; *The Man Who Shot Liberty Valance* (1962) as Kaintuck; *Cheyenne Autumn* (1964) as Texas cattle drover, Skinny.

Shug Fisher was born in rural Oklahoma, the youngest of four children. He got his nickname from his mother who called him Shug, short for sugar. As a child, Fisher was interested in music and learned to play numerous instruments. When he was sixteen, he watched a traveling medicine show and decided he wanted a life on stage. He traveled to California, sang and played his fiddle at dozens of square dances, and by the late 1920s was performing on radio. Throughout the 1930s, he played with various country

Shug Fisher

groups and in 1943 joined The Sons of the Pioneers. By then, his facial and stuttering comedy were a basic part of his repertoire.

Eventually, he followed his friend Ken Curtis into films and television. Fisher played numerous silly sidekicks and comic characters in B-westerns, and was the animated voice of Uncle Pecos in the 1955 cartoon, *Pecos Pest*.

In *The Man Who Shot Liberty Valance*, Fisher portrayed Kaintuck, a coonskinned drunk who is told he can't bring his jug to a political meeting. Like John Wayne's "good badman" in *3 Godfathers* carrying on the tradition of Harry Carey's Cheyenne Harry, and Mike Mazurki's Sgt. Wichowsky in *Cheyenne Autumn* taking over for Victor McLaglen's many sergeants, Kaintuck is a tribute to the many intoxicated and intoxicating characters that John Ford's older brother, Francis, had played in scores of motion pictures.

## Barry Fitzgerald

Barry Fitzgerald (1888-1961) appeared in five Ford productions: *The Plough and the Stars* (1936) as Fluther Good; *Four Men and a Prayer* (1938) as Trooper Mulcahay; *The Long Voyage Home* (1940) as Cocky; *How Green Was My Valley* (1941) as Cyfartha; *The Quiet Man* (1952) as Michaleen Oge Flynn.

He was born William Joseph Shields in Dublin, the older brother of fellow Ford company player, Arthur Shields. After an early career in civil service, the 5'3" Shields began acting with Dublin's famous Abbey Players and changed his name to Barry

Fitzgerald. According to Fitzgerald, his first speaking part was in Richard Sheridan's play, *The Critic*, and his first line was, "'Tis meet it should." The young, nervous novice mispronounced the phrase and loudly announced, "'Tis sheet it mould."

Barry Fitzgerald

He soon became a lead player, starring in Sean O'Casey's *Juno and the Paycock*, a role he repeated in Alfred Hitchcock's 1930 film. He appeared on Broadway in the early 1930s and then went to Hollywood to act for Ford in *The Plough and the Stars* in 1936. He won an Oscar as Best Supporting Actor for his most famous non-Ford role, Father Fitzgibbon, in *Going My Way* (1944).

Fitzgerald did admirable work in all five of his Ford movies but the first four characters were dwarfed by his Michaleen Oge Flynn in *The Quiet Man*. Still, his Cyfartha in *How Green Was My Valley* has one of the great lines in Ford films:

> Mr. Gruffydd (Walter Pidgeon): "Who is for Gwilym Morgan (Donald Crisp) and the others?"
> Dai Bando (Rhys Williams): "I, for one. He is the blood of my heart. Come, Cyfartha."
> Cyfartha: "'Tis a coward I am. But I will hold your coat."

Fitzgerald was one of Hollywood's most notorious scene stealers, and he most definitely was in his element in *The Quiet Man*. His sly looks, his double-takes, and his subtle gestures combined with Ford's blatant humor, particularly revolving around drinking, to offer the audience numerous treasured Fordian moments:

*Michaleen and Mary Kate (Maureen O'Hara) meet to discuss her dowry:*
Mary Kate: "Could you use a little water in your whiskey?"
Michaleen: "When I drink whiskey, I drink whiskey, and when I drink water, I drink water."

*When visiting the Squire's home, attempting to broker a marriage between Mary Kate and Sean (John Wayne):*
Michaleen: "I don't suppose there's a drop in the house."
Squire Danaher (Victor McLaglen): "Help yourself to the buttermilk."
Michaleen: "Buttermilk? The Borgias would do better."

*While chaperoning Mary Kate and Sean on their first official date:*
Michaleen: "Is this a courting or a donnybrook? Have the good manners not to hit the man until he's your husband and entitled to hit you back."

When Michaleen is chasing Sean and Mary Kate in his horse-drawn carriage, the horse instinctively stops in front of Cohan's Pub. Michaleen immediately compliments the horse, "I... I think you have more sense than I have me-self." The horse nods.

Finally, on seeing Sean and Mary Kate's broken marriage bed, Michaleen declares, "Impetuous! Homeric!"

**Charles Fitzsimons**

Charles Fitzsimons (1924-2001) appeared in three Ford productions: *What Price Glory* (1952) as Capt. Wickham; *The Quiet Man* (1952) as I.R.A. leader, Hugh Forbes; *The Last Hurrah* (1958) as Kevin McClusky.

He was born Charles B. FitzSimons in Ranelagh, Dublin, Ireland, the brother of stock company members Maureen O'Hara and James Lilburn. He

Charles Fitzsimons

earned a barrister-in-law degree and then acted with the Abbey Players in Dublin. In the early 1950s, he moved to America to manage his sister's career and find acting roles for himself in the movies. After a few credits as a supporting actor, he became a successful production supervisor beginning with the western, *The Deadly Companions* (1961), starring his sister, Maureen, and Brian Keith, and directed by Sam Peckinpah. He also produced episodes in such television series as *Love American Style* in 1969 and *Nanny and the Professor* in 1970. He was founder and executive director of the Producers Guild of America. Aka Charles FitzSimons, Charles B. Fitzsimons.

In *The Last Hurrah*, Fitzsimons does an excellent job depicting Kevin McClusky, an empty, vacillating, dim politician who defeats Spencer Tracy's incumbent. But it is his I.R.A. leader, Hugh Forbes, in *The Quiet Man* who has several notable Fordian moments.

Forbes makes a poignant toast at the wedding of Sean Thornton (John Wayne) and Mary Kate Danaher (Maureen O'Hara) with a little bit of politics thrown in:

"Then a toast. May their lives be long and full of happiness; may their children be many and full of health, and may they live in peace… and freedom."

Forbes has a succinct answer to Mary Kate's question about her husband:

"What manner of man is it that I have married?"
Forbes: "A better one, I think than you know, Mary Kate."

When the entire community appears at the farm of Squire Danaher (Victor McLaglen), Fitzsimons' character has another memorable reply to a Danaher question:

Red Will Danaher: "So the I.R.A.'s in this too, huh?"
Hugh Forbes: "If it were, Red Will Danaher, not a scorched stone 'o your fine house'd be standin'."

## James Flavin

James Flavin (1906-1976) appeared in eight Ford productions: *Airmail* (1932) man with radio report; *The Grapes of Wrath* (1940) guard; *The Long Voyage Home* (1940) dock policeman; *When Willie Comes Marching Home* (1950) as Gen. Brevort; *Mister Roberts* (1955) military policeman; *The Wings of Eagles* (1957) MP at garden party; *The Last Hurrah* (1958) as police captain, Michael J. Shanahan; *Cheyenne Autumn* (1964) sergeant of the guard at Ft. Robinson.

A tall, jut-jawed Irish-looking character actor (although he was actually only one-quarter Irish), James Flavin was born in Portland, Maine and attended West Point. In the late 1920s, he decided on an acting career and arrived in Hollywood in 1932. Within months, he was starring in his first movie, *The Airmail Mystery*, and marrying the leading lady, Lucile Brown. Although this was basically his only starring role, he was never out of a job as he played hundreds of tough, brash uniformed cops, police detectives, Marine sergeants, and city cabbies in over 400 films and television episodes. His last role was

James Flavin

as Dwight D. Eisenhower in the television drama, *Francis Gary Powers: The True Story of the U-2 Spy Incident* (1976). Three of his most well-known non-Ford parts were Second Mate Briggs in *King Kong* (1933), one of Errol Flynn's battling brothers in *Gentleman Jim* (1942), and the circus owner, Hoatley, who hires Tyrone Power's character in *Nightmare Alley* (1949).

Perhaps, because Flavin and John Ford shared Portland, Maine as their hometown, Ford continually found Flavin small parts. Over a thirty-two year period, Flavin worked for Ford in four separate decades, usually playing sarcastic policemen, laborers, or military men.

### Henry Fonda

Henry Fonda (1905-1982) participated in eight Ford productions: *Young Mr. Lincoln* (1939) as Abraham Lincoln; *Drums Along the Mohawk* (1939) as Gilbert Martin; *The Grapes of Wrath* (1940) as Tom Joad; the documentary, *The Battle of Midway* (1942) narrator; *My Darling Clementine* (1946) as Wyatt Earp; *The*

*Fugitive* (1947) the priest; *Fort Apache* (1948) as Lt. Col. Owen Thursday; *Mister Roberts* (1955) as Lt. JG Douglas A. Roberts.

Henry Fonda was born in Grand Island, Nebraska but grew up in Omaha. He attended the University of Minnesota for two years majoring in journalism and then dropped out to work. In 1925, he received a request that would change his life. Mrs. Dorothy Brando, the leader of Omaha's semi-professional theatrical group

(and the mother of one year-old Marlon) asked Fonda to try out for the juvenile lead in Philip Barry's play, *You and I.* The acting bug bit and within a few years, he was acting at the Cape Playhouse in Cape Cod with such future luminaries as his future first wife Margaret Sullivan, Joshua Logan, and a gangly string bean named Jimmy Stewart. After almost a decade of apprenticeships and failures, he finally achieved

Henry Fonda

success in 1934 starring in Broadway's *The Farmer Takes a Wife.* In early 1935, he arrived in Hollywood and began filming *The Farmer Takes a Wife.* His engaging sincerity combined with his relaxed style of delivery proved ideal for the screen and he soon became a major movie star. He made films for almost fifty years, occasionally venturing back to Broadway or into television. Among his many notable non-Ford films were *The Lady Eve* (1941), *The Big Street* (1942), *The Wrong Man* (1956), *Twelve Angry Men* (1957), *Fail Safe* (1964), and *On Golden Pond* (1981) for which he won the Best Actor Academy Award. He was the father of Jane and Peter Fonda, significant Hollywood players in the 1960s and 1970s.

Henry Fonda's seven characters for John Ford were each unforgettable, courageous men who, with one exception (Lt. Colonel Owen Thursday in *Fort Apache*), demonstrate their integrity by fighting their battles against injustice, evil, and oppression. Ford used Fonda's innate integrity, his quiet strength of character, and even the hint of awkwardness in his physical bearing to create people who are etched in our minds and memories.

In *Young Mr. Lincoln*, Ford and Fonda sum up the entire American legal system in three words:

> "By jing, that's all there is to it: Right and Wrong."

In *Drums Along the Mohawk*, a shattered Gil returns from the Battle of Oriskany and numbly relates to Lara his experiences at war.

In *The Grapes of Wrath*, there's THE conversation between Ma (Jane Darwell) and Tom:

> Ma: "How am I gonna know about ya, Tommy? Why they could kill ya and I'd never know. They could hurt ya. How am I gonna know?"
> Tom: "Well, maybe it's like Casey says. A fellow ain't got a soul of his own, just a little piece of a big soul, the one big soul that belongs to everybody, then…"
> Ma: "Then what, Tommy?"
> Tom: "Then it don't matter. I'll be all around in the dark—I'll be everywhere. Wherever you can look—wherever there's a fight, so hungry people can eat, I'll be there. Wherever there's a cop beatin' up a guy, I'll be there. I'll be in the way guys yell when they're mad. I'll be in the way kids laugh when they're hungry and they

know supper's ready, and when the people are eatin' the stuff they raise and livin' in the houses they build–I'll be there, too."

In *My Darling Clementine*, there is the unforgettable scene when Marshal Wyatt Earp dances with his ladyfair (Cathy Downs) celebrating the first church of Tombstone. In this perfect example of Ford's sparse yet rich direction, Henry Fonda's Wyatt Earp displays several unexpected character traits for a legendary western hero: initial shyness, physical awkwardness, and his desire to participate in such a public social occasion. But as the scene evolves, one can see Wyatt relax and his dancing improves, so by the end of the dance, he is almost graceful.

In *The Fugitive*, there is a scene when Fonda's priest sits with a doctor and is visibly uncomfortable and physically drained. Fonda later related that he felt physically ill playing the role. As he had done with other actors in other movies (Victor McLaglen in *The Informer* and Woody Strode in *Sergeant Rutledge*), John Ford may have deliberately set up the actor's discomfort to capture the character's angst.

In *Fort Apache*, for the first time in his career, Fonda portrayed an unpleasant character, a rigid, arrogant martinet who eventually leads his troops into an utter defeat. But Ford found a comical moment for even this serious, inflexible army officer when Colonel Thursday's chair collapses beneath him.

In *Mister Roberts*, Fonda's Doug Roberts is extremely poised, balanced, and controlled until his frustration with the ship's Captain (James Cagney) erupts, and in an unforgettable serious and silly scene, he tosses the Captain's beloved palm tree into the sea.

## Francis Ford

Francis Ford (1881-1953) appeared in thirty-one Ford productions: *Action* (1921) as Soda Water Manning; *The Village Blacksmith* (1922) as Asa Martin; *Three Jumps Ahead* (1923) as Ben McLean; *Hearts of Oak* (1924) bit; *The Fighting Heart* (1925) town fool; *Upstream* (1927) juggler; *The Black Watch* (1929) as Major MacGregor; *Seas Beneath* (1931) as captain of trawler, Eric; *Airmail* (1931) passenger; *Pilgrimage* (1933) as Mayor Elmer Briggs; *Doctor Bull* (1933) meeting chairman, Mr. Herring; *The Lost Patrol* (1934) Arab; *The World Moves On* (1934) legionnaire in trench; *Judge Priest* (1934) juror #12; *The Whole Town's Talking* (1935) newspaper reporter at dock; *The Informer* (1935) as "Judge" Flynn; *Steamboat Round the Bend* (1935) as Efe; *The Prisoner of Shark Island* (1936) as Cpl. O'Toole; *The Plough and the Stars* (1936) bit;

Francis Ford

*Stagecoach* (1939) as Billy Pickett; *Young Mr. Lincoln* (1939) as Sam Boone; *Drums Along the Mohawk* (1939) as Joe Boleo; *The Grapes of Wrath* (1940) bit; *Tobacco Road* (1941) vagabond on the road; *My Darling Clementine* (1946) as old soldier, Old Dad; *Fort Apache* (1948) as Fen; *3 Godfathers* (1948) drunken old-timer; *She Wore a Yellow Ribbon* (1949) as barman "Irish" Connelly; *Wagon Master* (1950) as Mr. Peachtree; *The Quiet Man* (1952) as Dan Tobin; *The Sun Shines Bright* (1953) as Finney.

Francis Ford, John Ford's older brother, was born Frank Thomas Feeney in Portland, Maine. After several years of stage acting, he began working for Gaston Méliès' U.S.-based company, then for the New York Motion Picture Company under Thomas Ince, and eventually for Universal in 1913. At Universal, he directed and starred in numerous silent serials, many with his co-star and co-writer, Grace Cunard. Beginning in 1914, he mentored his brother, John, for three years before the younger brother began directing on his own in 1917. Francis continued directing until 1928, when his drinking and lack of discipline thwarted his career, and he turned to character acting.

Francis Ford's characters in his brother's films are usually remembered as good-natured *Informer* certainly abuses his authority. But it is his old-timers who added so much comedy and pathos (in so little screen time with so little dialogue) that were his biggest contribution to Ford's films and his company.

In *Steamboat Round the Bend*, he played Efe, a good-natured drunk who is continually making the pledge to abstain from alcohol:

> "The New Moses" (Berton Churchill): "Raise your right hand and take the pledge. Brother, what do I see in your hand? Don't be a hog. Cast the enemy away! Bury demon rum in the waters of the mighty Mississippi! Fling it away, I say! I swear henceforth, liquor shall never touch my lips."
> Efe: "Me too."

In *She Wore a Yellow Ribbon*, he played the barman, "Irish" Connelly, who commiserates and reminisces with Sgt. Quincannon (Victor McLaglen) before and during yet another Fordian bar brawl.

In *The Quiet Man*, his most famous scene occurs when his dying old man leaps out of his deathbed to witness the fight between

Sean (John Wayne) and Danaher (Victor McLaglen). But earlier in the film, in the crowded pub, his Dan Tobin monopolizes the scene. After the Squire's man (Jack MacGowran) announces that Danaher has the floor, Tobin brandishes his cane and declares, "If I had the floor, I'd hit that big ape with it!" and proceeds to grab the audience's eye throughout the rest of the scene.

In *The Sun Shines Bright*, he played Brother Finney, the final reincarnation of the fun-loving, hard-drinking grizzled veteran. There is a camera shot of the drunk, good-natured Finney with a jug he had snuck into a temperance ladies' dance happily drinking away under the campaign banner, "Maydew will drive out the Moonshiners!"

## Wallace Ford

Wallace Ford (1898-1966) appeared in four Ford productions: *The Lost Patrol* (1934) as Morelli; *The Whole Town's Talking* (1935) as Healy; *The Informer* (1935) as Frankie McPhillip; *The Last Hurrah* (1958) as Charles J. Hennessey.

Wallace Ford was born Samuel Jones Grundy in Lancashire, England and grew up in an orphanage and foster homes. (In the mid-1930s, he connected with his actual parents). At eleven, he ran away from his foster home in Canada to join a vaudeville troupe.

For a while, he traveled the rails with a friend named Wallace Ford who was crushed to death in a

Wallace Ford

train accident. To honor his friend, Grundy changed his name to Wallace Ford. Eventually, he turned to acting on stage as his career.

After some success starring in several Broadway productions, he ventured to Hollywood in 1930 and the next year had a choice role as the other guy in *Possessed* (1931), starring Joan Crawford and Clark Gable. For the next three-and-a-half decades, he appeared in over 200 films and television shows, initially appearing as affable tough guys, and later in his career, as fatherly types. He was a regular on Henry Fonda's western series, *The Deputy* (1959-1960). His last movie role was Ole Pa in *A Patch of Blue* (1965).

According to John Ford, Wallace Ford had a significant role in *They Were Expendable* as a priest that was later cut out by M-G-M. Like many of Ford's stock company players, his parts, though never substantial, added balance, substance, and texture to a movie. And in *The Informer*, the plot revolves around the betrayal and death of his Irish Republican martyr, Frankie McPhillip.

**Earle Foxe**

Earle Foxe (1887-1973) appeared in six Ford productions: *Upstream* (1927) as Eric Brasingham; *Hangman's House* (1928) as John D'Arcy; *Four Sons* (1928) as Maj. von Stomm; *The Informer*

(1935) British officer; *Mary of Scotland* (1936) as the Earl of Kent; *My Darling Clementine* (1946) gambler run out of town by Doc Holliday.

Born Earl Aldrich Fox in Ohio, he attended Ohio State University before doing theatrical and film acting in New York. He was the lead in Cecil B. DeMille's *Trail of the Lonesome Pine* (1916). He came to Hollywood in 1922, signed with

Earle Foxe

Fox, and began a long career that lasted until the mid-1940s. He was one of the founders of the Black-Foxe Military Institute, a private military school located in Hollywood. For many years, Earle Foxe served as president of the school which Ford's son, Patrick, and Harry Carey Jr. attended.

John Ford's films seldom had extremely vile villains, but two of Foxe's antagonists were despicable men. In *Hangsman's House*, his scoundrel D'Arcy kills Fighting Hogan's (Victor McLaglen) sister and manipulates an innocent girl into marriage so he can steal her estate. In *Four Sons*, his Major von Stomm is the ultimate Nazi before there were Nazis. His cowardly, cheating gambler in *My Darling Clementine* is a laudable fellow by comparison.

### Neva Gerber

Neva Gerber (1894-1974) appeared in four Ford productions: *Hell Bent* (1918) as Bess Thurston; *Three Mounted Men* (1918) as Lola Masters; *Roped* (1919) as Aileen; *A Fight for Love* (1919) as Kate McDougal.

She was born in Chicago but moved to Los Angeles after her parents separated. After high school, she began acting. She made her film debut in the one-reeler *Flower Girl*

Neva Gerber

in 1912. She joined Universal in 1916 and teamed with actor/director Ben Wilson in nine serials beginning with *The Mystery Ship* (1917) and ending with the first sound serial, *The Voice from the Sky* (1930). During the 1920s, she was a very popular movie star and was engaged, for a while, to the ill-fated director, William

Desmond Taylor, who was found murdered in February of 1922. Aka Jean Dolores.

In the late 'teens, during her early years at Universal, Neva Gerber acted for Ford on four Harry Carey silent westerns, playing the female lead when Molly Malone was unavailable. Due to her experience in filmmaking and her professionalism, she was never a prima donna and worked well with Ford, Harry Carey, and the rest of the early company.

## Bill Gettinger/Bill Steel

Bill Gettinger/Bill Steel (1888-1966) appeared in nine Ford productions: *The Soul Herder* (1917) bit; *Cheyenne's Pal* (1917) cowboy; *The Secret Man* (1917) foreman; *A Marked Man* (1917) sheriff; *Bucking Broadway* (1917) as Buck Hoover; *The Phantom Riders* (1917) as Dave Bland; *The Wallop* (1921) as Christopher Foy; *She Wore a Yellow Ribbon* (1949) trooper; *The Searchers* (1955) as Nesby.

Bill Gettinger/Bill Steel

He was born William Anton Gettinger in San Antonio, Texas. He arrived in Los Angeles in 1910 and worked in silent westerns until World War I service, when he fought in Europe. After he returned to the United States—and to making westerns again—he found consistent work for over thirty years. During these years, he made countless B-westerns and serials and occasionally had parts in such well-known westerns as Jimmy Stewart's *Destry Rides Again* (1939), Howard Hughes and Jane Russell's *The Outlaw* (1943), and Errol Flynn's *San Antonio* (1945). Aka Bill Gettenger, Bill Gitenger, William Steel, Bill Steuer.

Bill Gettinger/Bill Steel made five early Ford films and was an active member of Ford's initial company, working closely with Harry Carey and Vester Pegg not only in Ford's westerns but also in other Universal oaters directed by Fred Kelsey. After a hiatus of almost thirty years, he worked for Ford again in *She Wore a Yellow Ribbon* under the name Bill Steele. Even though he was sixty years old, his cavalry trooper showed remarkable riding skills and vigor. In *The Searchers*, his character, Nesby, the neighbor/posse member who is wounded at the battle with the Comanches at the river, appears to be more upset with the foolish Mose Harper (Hank Worden) than he is with the Indians or his wound.

## Hoot Gibson

Hoot Gibson (1892-1962) appeared in thirteen Ford productions: *The Soul Herder* (1917) bit; *Cheyenne's Pal* (1917) cowboy; *Straight Shooting* (1917) as Danny Morgan; *The Secret Man* (1917) as Chuck Fadden; *A Marked Man* (1917) bit; *The Fighting Brothers* (1919) as Lonnie Larkin; *By Indian Post* (1919) as Jode's cowboy friend, Chub; *The Rustlers* (1919) deputy; *Gun Law* (1919) as Bart "Smoke Gublen" Stevens; *The Gun Packer* (1919) gang leader; *Action* (1921) as Sandy Brourke; *Sure Fire* (1921) as Jeff Bransford; *The Horse Soldiers* (1959) as Sgt. Brown.

He was born Edmund Richard Gibson in Tekamah, Nebraska, had his first pony at two, and moved to California with his family when he was seven years old. There were numerous rationalizations for his nickname; the fact that he liked to hunt owls as a boy is as good as any. When he was a teenager, he ran away from home to join the circus, and then quickly became a cowboy and a rodeo performer in wild west shows. By the time he was twenty in

1912, he was crowned "The World's Champion Cowboy" at the Pendleton, Oregon Roundup. That same year, he began his film career, working as an extra and a stuntman. He soon was doubling for many of the western movie stars including Harry Carey. He was doing supporting roles for Ford when he joined the army to fight in World War I.

After his service, Gibson returned to Hollywood, and by 1921 he was starring in his own feature westerns under Ford. By the mid-

Hoot Gibson

1920s, riding his palomino, Goldie, Hoot Gibson had become one of the most popular silent western stars, often utilizing a humorous slant. In 1930, he was let go by Universal and spent the next fifteen years working on and off in B-westerns. He was married four times, three times to actresses: Helen Gibson, Sally Eilers, and Dorothea Dunstan.

In the mid-'teens, Gibson roomed with Ford in an apartment on Hollywood Boulevard. After several years of support work, Gibson starred in the silent western *Action*, which was Francis Ford's first John Ford-directed movie. Gibson also starred in Ford's *Sure Fire*, and then Ford moved to Fox and Hoot moved up to major cowboy stardom. Almost forty years later, Ford helped Gibson out financially by getting him a small role as a veteran sergeant in *The Horse Soldiers* at a salary of $5,000.

Hoot Gibson's work in *Straight Shooting* was representative of the "aw shucks" goodtime cowboy roles he usually played. In this Harry Carey/Cheyenne Harry silent western and John Ford's first feature, Gibson is Danny Morgan, a cowboy torn by his loyalty to his rancher boss (Duke R. Lee) and his love for a farmer's daughter (Molly Malone). In the movie, Hoot demonstrates deft riding ability and a knack for comedy. There is a scene in which he's riding his horse across a river, the horse slips, and Gibson falls off the horse. He immediately jumps back on and away they gallop.

## Mary Gordon

Mary Gordon (1882-1963) appeared in ten Ford productions: *Hangman's House* (1928) woman at Hogan's Hideout; *The Black Watch* (1929) Sandy's wife; *Pilgrimage* (1933) as Mrs. MacGregor; *Doctor Bull* (1933) townswoman at meeting; *The World Moves On* (1934) English soldier's mother; *The Whole Town's Talking* (1935) bit; *Mary of Scotland* (1936) nurse; *The Plough and the Stars* (1936) as woman at the barricades, Doris Lloyd; *How Green Was My Valley* (1941) gossiper; *Fort Apache* (1948) as Ma.

Mary Gordon was born Mary Gilmour in Glasgow, Scotland in 1882 and began touring with several singing troupes as a young girl. She eventually landed in Los Angeles in the 1920s and appeared in her first film, the drama *The Home Maker*

Mary Gordon

staring Clive Brook, in 1925. For over twenty years, she had small parts in films, usually as a domestic, mother, or housekeeper. In 1939, she played literature and film's most famous housekeeper, Mrs. Hudson, in the Sherlock Holmes mystery, *The Hound of the*

*Baskervilles*, the first of ten movies she made with Basil Rathbone and Nigel Bruce.

In the motion pictures she made for John Ford, all of her parts were small, but certain scenes with her linger.

In *The World Moves On*, she offers motherly advice to her English soldier son (Ben Hall):

"Don't let the other soldiers coax you to take whiskey!"

John Ford's movies are filled with alliteration in his dialogue. For example, in *Fort Apache*, Gordon's friendly neighbor compliments the hat worn by the young colonel's daughter, Philadelphia (Shirley Temple):

"Oh, my, that's a real bonny bonnet, miss."

## Fred Graham

Fred Graham (1908-1979) appeared in five Ford productions: *Fort Apache* (1948) cavalryman; *She Wore a Yellow Ribbon* (1949) as Sgt. Hench; *When Willie Comes Marching Home* (1950) male nurse; *The Wings of Eagles* (1957) officer in brawl; *The Horse Soldiers* (1959) Union soldier.

Fred Graham

Graham was born in Springer, New Mexico and was always an excellent athlete. When he was twenty, he was playing semi-pro baseball and working in the M-G-M sound department when he was asked to help Robert Young and Nat Pendleton look like authentic ballplayers for the mystery, *Death on the Diamond* (1934). For the next forty years, "Slugger" worked as a stuntman, an extra, and as a double for such stars as Clark Gable in

*Mutiny on the Bounty* (1935), Nelson Eddy in *Rose-Marie* (1936), and Basil Rathbone in *The Adventures of Robin Hood* (1937). His specialty was fist fights and Graham was a master at making the fake look real. Western and action director William Witney proclaimed Graham, "the best screen brawler I ever used." Graham participated in two classic non-Ford fracases, the barroom brawl in Errol Flynn's *Dodge City* (1939) and the fight with John Wayne in *Seven Sinners* (1940).

But it is his participation in *She Wore a Yellow Ribbon's* fisticuffs between Sgt. Quincannon (Victor McLaglen) and six soldiers in the bar that will always be remembered.

After Graham's Sgt. Hench announces, "I'd love to throw that big Mick into the cooler," he joins Sgt. Hochbauer (Michael Dugan), the blacksmith Wagner (Mickey Simpson), Badger (Fred Kennedy) and two others in an over-the-top brawl that has been a guilty pleasure for generations of audiences.

## Charlie Grapewin

Charlie Grapewin (1869-1956) appeared in four Ford productions: *Pilgrimage* (1933) as Dad Saunders; *Judge Priest* (1934) as Sgt. Jimmy Bagby; *The Grapes of Wrath* (1940) as Grandpa Joad; *Tobacco Road* (1941) as Jeeter Lester.

Born in Xenia, Ohio, Grapewin worked in circuses as a trapeze artist, in vaudeville, and on the stage, often in productions that he wrote. He married Anna Chance in 1895 and they were a couple until her death in 1943. In 1929, when he was sixty years old, he made his first feature movie, a comedy starring James Gleason titled *The Shannons of Broadway*. During the next twenty years, he made over 100 motion pictures, usually playing wise and crusty old codgers. Notable non-Ford roles included the old father in Paul Muni and Luise Rainer's *The Good Earth* (1937); Dorothy's

(Judy Garland) Uncle Henry in *The Wizard of Oz* (1939); old-timer California Joe in Errol Flynn's *They Died with Their Boots On* (1941), and Inspector Queen in seven Ellery Queen mysteries during the early 1940s.

Charlie Grapewin

Grapewin's first two Fordian characters were dwarfed by the latter two, but each was distinctive in different ways. His Dad Sanders in *Pilgrimage* demonstrates substantial strength and courage when he forcibly tells Hannah (Henrietta Crossman) that she must help deliver her grandchild: "This ain't no time to quarrel, Hannah." In *Judge Priest*, his Sgt. Bagby is an alcoholic obsessed with his past, namely his alleged heroics during the Civil War.

In *The Grapes of Wrath*, Grapewin plays Grandpa Joad, a victim to events he has absolutely no control over. John Qualen's Muhey's emotional scene with the Caterpillar tractor is much more famous, but Grandpa unwillingness to leave his land is equally as wrenching and powerful:

"It's my dirt! Eh-heh! No good, but it's mine, all mine."

In *Tobacco Road*, Grapewin's performance is exceptional; one can empathize with Jeeter's sadness over the ruined lives of his children, be upset with his selfish ruthlessness, and respect his refusal to bow to unwanted changes.

Jeeter is the core of this comedy/tragedy. He is both a man of low comedy and great sadness. He can jokingly remember, "Why, Ada (Elizabeth Patterson) here never... never spoke a word to me for the first ten years we were married. Heh! Them was the happiest years of my life," and then become almost despondent, "All that they were, and all that they had, is gone with the wind and the dust."

## Ben Hall

Ben Hall (1899-1985) appeared in eight Ford productions: *Salute* (1929) as Midshipman Joel Farragut Gish; *Seas Beneath* (1931) as Elmer Harrigan; *The World Moves On* (1934) English soldier; *Steamboat Round the Bend* (1935) Fleety Belle's brother; *The Plough and the Stars* (1936) bit; *The Grapes of Wrath* (1940) gas station attendant in Bakersfield; *How Green Was My Valley* (1941) bit; *My Darling Clementine* (1946) barber.

Ben Hall

Hall was born in Brooklyn, New York and began acting in silent shorts in the New York metropolitan area when he was a child. By 1920, he had moved to Los Angeles and worked first as a property man for several studios and then, gradually, found regular roles in early talkies. Over the next twenty years, he appeared in over 150 movies.

Hall's small roles with Ford were basically bits, but one of his characters is truly memorable, the nervous but efficient little barber in *My Darling Clementine*.

## Charles Halton

Charles Halton (1876-1959) appeared in four Ford productions: *Young Mr. Lincoln* (1939) as Hawthorne; *Tobacco Road* (1941) mayor; *3 Godfathers* (1948) as bank president,

Charles Halton

Oliver Latham; *When Willie Comes Marching Home* (1950) as Mr. Fettles.

He was born in Washington, D.C. and trained at the New York Academy of Dramatic Arts. He acted with touring companies and on Broadway before becoming a character actor in Hollywood for twenty-five years, beginning in 1931. He was a small, stern-faced man who usually played bespeckled, officious characters. Three of his most typical and best-remembered non-Ford roles were the suspicious doctor in the Marx Brothers' *Room Service* (1938), the harried stage producer in Jack Benny and Carole Lombard's *To Be or Not to Be* (1942), and the somber bank examiner in Frank Capra's *It's a Wonderful Life* (1946).

In Ford's films, Charles Halton is best remembered as the uncompromising farmer in *Young Mr. Lincoln* who goes to the young lawyer (Henry Fonda) to settle a dispute with an equally stern-faced neighbor, Russell Simpson's Woolridge, and as the humorless bank president in *3 Godfathers*.

## Joe Harris

Joe Harris (1870-1953) appeared in fourteen Ford productions: *Hell Bent* (1918) as outlaw Beau Ross; *Three Mounted Men* (1918) as Buck Masters; *A Fight for Love* (1919) as Black Michael; *Bare Fists* (1919) as Boone Travis; *Riders of Vengeance* (1919) as Sheriff Gale Thurman; *The Outcasts of Poker Flat* (1919) as Ned Stratton; *The Ace of the Saddle* (1919) Yucca County sheriff ; *The Rider of the Law* (1919) as Buck Soutar; *A Gun Fightin' Gentleman* (1919) as Seymour; *Marked Men* (1919) as Tom Gibbons; *Hitchin' Posts* (1920) as Louis Castigo; *The Freeze-Out* (1920) as Headlight Whipple; *The Wallop* (1920) as Barela; *Sure Fire* (1921) as Romero.

Joe Harris was born in Lewiston, Maine of Irish stock. After a variety of jobs as a young man, he made his way to California and by 1914 he was acting in small parts in silent shorts such as *Withering Roses*, *Fooling Uncle*, and *Bess, the Outcast*. By the time he made his first film with Ford, he was a veteran of almost fifty films. Aka Joseph Harris.

Joe Harris

Harris and Harry Carey were close friends; Harris met John Ford through Carey. Harris was an active member of the early Ford-Carey company. The dark-haired Harris usually played scowling villains but occasionally was cast as a lawman. Harris lived with Harry and Olive Carey on their ranch on and off for many years and died there. It appears that his gossiping about Ford to Carey may have contributed to Ford and Carey's disassociation after making *Desperate Trails* together in June 1921.

## Sam Harris

Sam Harris (1877-1969) appeared in eleven Ford productions: *The Informer* (1935) British officer; *When Willie Comes Marching Home* (1950) hospital patient; *The Quiet Man* (1952) as the General; *The Wings of Eagles* (1957) patient; *The Last Hurrah* (1958) member of the Plymouth Club; *The Horse Soldiers* (1959) as Major Newton Townsman; *Sergeant Rutledge* (1960) courtroom spectator; *Two Rode Together* (1961) army post doctor; *The Man*

Sam Harris

*Who Shot Liberty Valance* (1962) convention committee member; *Donovan's Reef* (1963) family council member; *Cheyenne Autumn* (1964) Dodge City townsman.

Harris was born in Sydney, Australia and eventually arrived in Hollywood where he had his first role in the thriller *The Spirit of Gallipoli* (1928) as William Austin. It was one of the few times he had a role with a name. For the next forty-eight years, Harris had small parts as party guests, spectators, older faces in the crowd, and various other extras in over 500 motion pictures and television episodes. Along with Franklyn Farnum, Bess Flowers, and Wallis Clark, he is the only actor to have appeared in five Best Picture Academy Award winners; he had small parts in *You Can't Take It With You* (1938) *All the King's Men*, (1949), *Around the World in Eighty Days* (1956), *My Fair Lady* (1964), and *The Sound of Music* (1965).

There can be no argument as to his best bit in a Ford film: his General sitting silently in Cohan's pub totally oblivious to the fight between Sean (John Wayne) and Danaher (Victor McLaglen) in *The Quiet Man.*

## Chuck Hayward

Chuck Hayward (1920-1998) appeared in thirteen Ford productions: *She Wore a Yellow Ribbon* (1949) bit; *Wagon Master* (1950) as Sam Jenkins; *Rio Grande* (1950) bit; *The Sun Shines Bright* (1953) bit; *The Searchers* (1956) man at wedding; *The Wings of Eagles* (1957) bit; *The Horse Soldiers* (1959) Union captain;

*Sergeant Rutledge* (1960) bit; *The Colter Craven Story* episode from television's *Wagon Train* series (1960) as Quentin Cleatus; *Two Rode Together* (1961) trooper; *The Man Who Shot Liberty Valance* (1962) henchman; *Cheyenne Autumn* (1964) bit; *7 Women* (1966) bit.

Hayward was born on a ranch outside of Hyannis, Nebraska where his parents raised horses. After attending college, serving in the Merchant Marines during World War II, and participating in rodeo competitions, he moved to California in 1947 and attempted to get into the film business. In 1949, he was hired for stunt work in John Wayne's *The Fighting Kentuckian*. He and Wayne became good friends and

Chuck Hayward

he made twenty-four motion pictures with the Duke. He doubled for many of the stars of the 1950s, 1960s, and 1970s, including Richard Widmark, Yul Brynner, Steve McQueen, Gregory Peck, Clint Eastwood, and Burt Reynolds.

Through his friendship with Wayne, Hayward began to do stunts and bit parts in John Ford's films, beginning with *She Wore a Yellow Ribbon*. Ford called him "Good Chuck" in contrast to Chuck Roberson's "Bad Chuck" who had a more troublesome reputation. When Ford appeared on the television special, *Wide Wide World: The Western*, Hayward and his favorite horse, Twinkle Toes, demonstrated his expertise with stunt riding and falls.

One of Hayward's most noticeable roles was his Union officer in *The Horse Soldiers* who rides a horse into a saloon and then is quickly thrown out by John Wayne's angry colonel.

## William Henry

William Henry (1914-1982) appeared in twelve Ford productions: *Four Men and a Prayer* (1938) as Rodney Leigh; *What Price Glory* (1952) as Holsen; *Mister Roberts* (1955) as Lt. Billings; *The Wings of Eagles* (1957) naval aide; *The Last Hurrah* (1958) tallyman; *The Horse Soldiers* (1959) Confederate lieutenant; *Sergeant Rutledge* (1960) as Capt. Dwyer; *The Colter Craven Story* episode from television's *Wagon Train* series (1960) as Krindle; *Two Rode Together* (1961) gambler; *The Man Who Shot Liberty Valance*

William Henry

(1962) bit; *Flashing Spikes* episode from television's *Alcoa Premier* series (1962) assistant commissioner; *Cheyenne Autumn* (1964) infantry captain.

Henry was born in Los Angeles and worked as a child and juvenile player, a B-movie leading man, and a character actor in over 200 films and television episodes between 1925 and 1978. He made his movie debut when he was eight as a street urchin in *Lord Jim* (1925). In 1934, he played one of his most remembered roles, Gilbert Wynant, an obnoxious teenager and expectant heir in William Powell's *The Thin Man*. His foster brother was the famous Hawaiian athlete, Duke Kathanamoku. Henry was an excellent swimmer and diver, which he demonstrated in *Mister Roberts*. Aka Bill Henry.

His first role for Ford was a callow Oxford student, Rodney Leigh, the youngest of the four brothers searching for answers to the death of their father (C. Aubrey Smith) in *Four Men and a*

*Prayer;* his last was a bit part as an infantry captain in *Cheyenne Autumn* twenty six years later.

Observing Henry's work with Ford, as with many members of the company from Frank Albertson to John Wayne, Roger Greenspun's quotation used in this book's Introduction comes to mind:

"Some of them grew up with Ford; some grew old with him."

## Robert Homans

Robert Homans (1877-1947) appeared in eleven Ford productions: *Born Reckless* (1930) policeman; *The Whole Town's Talking* (1935) detective; *The Informer* (1935) detractor; *Steamboat Round the Bend* (1935) race official; *The Prisoner of Shark Island* (1936) sergeant; *Mary of Scotland* (1936) jailer; *The Plough and the Stars* (1936) as Timmy the Barman; *Stagecoach* (1939) as Ed; *Young Mr. Lincoln* (1939) as Mr. Clay; *The Grapes of Wrath* (1940) as Spencer; *They Were Expendable* (1945) bartender at Manila hotel.

Robert Homans

Robert Edward Homans was born in Malden, Massachusetts. After working in films in the New York City area, he moved to Los Angeles in 1923 and began an active acting career there. Between 1923 and 1946, the serious-looking Homans had bits and character roles in over 350 motion pictures, often portraying judges and policemen.

For Ford, Homans played an Irish detective in *The Whole Town's Talking*; a Southern official in *Steamboat Round the Bend*; an immoral huckster in a convertible looking to take advantage of migrant workers in *The Grapes of Wrath*, and a rural innocent, honest and earnest, who barters away Blackstone's *Commentaries* in *Young Mr. Lincoln*, and made each of these roles believable.

### Jeffrey Hunter

Jeffrey Hunter (1926-1969) appeared in three Ford productions: *The Searchers* (1955) as Martin Pawley; *The Last Hurrah* (1958) as Adam Caulfield; *Sergeant Rutledge* (1960) as Lt. Tom Cantrell.

He was born Henry Herman McKinnies in New Orleans, Louisiana, an only child. His family moved to Milwaukee in 1930 and he grew up in Wisconsin. He began acting with regional theater troupes and on a local radio station while in

Jeffrey Hunter

high school, and after service in the U.S. Navy from 1945-1946, attended Northwestern University in Evanston, Illinois, graduating in 1949. One of his classmates was Charlton Heston; both acted in the 1950 David Bradley film version of Shakespeare's *Julius Caesar*.

In 1950, while a graduate student at UCLA, Hunter was offered a contract from 20th Century-Fox. He made his film debut in 1951 in the Betty Grable/Dan Daily musical, *Call Me Mister*, and had his first starring vehicle in the 1953 World War II drama, *Sailor of the King*. He made over sixty-five movies and television episodes, and portrayed Jesus in Nicholas Ray's *King of Kings* (1961). He starred in his own western series, *Temple Houston* (1963-1964), and was the original captain of *The USS Enterprise* in *The Cage* (1964), the pilot television episode of *Star Trek*. His first wife was actress Barbara Rush; his last was actress Emily McLaughlin.

Hunter's three films with Ford demonstrate his growth as an actor. His Martin Pawley in *The Searchers* is a whipping-boy for John Wayne's Ethan Edwards during most of the movie; but by the end, Pawley has grown in stature and self-confidence to be an equal to Wayne's larger-than-life character. After their odyssey together, one could see John Wayne's older searcher turning to Marty, offering his hand, and stating, as Wayne's character did in *Red River* to another surrogate son, "You earned it."

In *The Last Hurrah*, Hunter's Adam Caulfield is a complex character. Caulfield is the sportswriter nephew of Mayor Frank Skeffington (Spencer Tracy) and is shown to be a bright, perceptive individual who values tradition and loyalty, rare traits for a young man in Ford's later films. But he is also arrogant, condescending, and never commits himself to a cause.

In each of Jeffrey Hunter's three Ford films, his characters could have easily been overshadowed by the actors he was playing against. In *The Searchers* and in *The Last Hurrah*, he shared most of his scenes with John Wayne and Spencer Tracy, merely two of the most powerful presences in Hollywood history. In *Sergeant Rutledge*, he co-starred with Woody Strode, who delivered the most forceful and charismatic role of his career. But like his characters in his first two Ford films, Hunter's Lt. Tom Cantrell demonstrates a variety of strong traits such as loyalty, bravery, competence, ingenuity, and intelligence, and again proves that actor Jeffrey Hunter was much more than just another pretty face.

### Brandon Hurst

Brandon Hurst (1866-1947) appeared in seven Ford productions: *Lightnin'* (1925) as Everette Hammond; *The Shamrock Handicap* (1926) procurer of taxes; *The Lost Patrol* (1934) as Bell; *Mary of Scotland* (1936) as Arian; *The Plough and the Stars* (1936) as Sgt. Tinley; *Wee Willie Winkie* (1937) as Bagby; *Four Men and a Prayer* (1938) jury foreman.

Hurst was born in London in 1866. As a student, he specialized in philology, the study of language in written historical sources; but by the late 1880s, he had turned to acting. He performed on stage and then in films. His first movie appearance was in the silent, *Via Wireless* (1916). In numerous silent films, Hurst specialized in playing villains such as the evil Sir George Carew in John Barrymore's *Dr. Jekyl and Mr.*

Brandon Hurst

*Hyde* (1920); Quasimodo's cruel master, Jehan, in Lon Chaney's *The Hunchback of Notre Dame* (1923), and the caliph in Douglas Fairbanks's *The Thief of Bagdad* (1924). His roles in talkies were usually less substantial.

The seven roles Hurst played in Ford's films were small but singular. In *The Lost Patrol*, his wounded soldier, Bell, tended by a crazed zealot (Boris Karloff), is quite convincing; but his most memorable role for Ford was, surprisingly, a humorous bit in *Wee Willie Winkie* as Bagby, the put-upon adjutant to the colonel (C. Aubrey Smith).

## Warren Hymer

Warren Hymer (1906-1948) appeared in five Ford productions: *Men Without Women* (1930) as Kaufman; *Born Reckless* (1930) as Big Shot; *Up The River* (1930) as Dannemora Dan; *Seas Beneath* (1931) as Lug Kaufman; *Submarine Patrol* (1938) as seaman Rocky Haggerty.

Hymer was born in New York City, the son of playwright John B. Hymer, author of nine Broadway productions during the first third of the twentieth century, including *East is East* (1918-1920), and *Aloma of the South Seas* (1925) that was made into a film starring John Hall and Dorothy Lamour. Warren Hymer graduated from Yale University and acted on Broadway before arriving in Hollywood in 1928.

During the 1930s, with his square chin, close-set eyes, and burly physique, Warren Hymer played scores of fast-talking sidekicks or dim-witted and good-natured characters on both sides of the law. According to Hollywood legend, Warren Hymer once was so angry at Columbia studio boss Harry Cohn for tossing him off the set when Hymer arrived intoxicated, that he urinated on Cohn's desk.

Warren Hymer

Ford was adept at using humorous characters in his films to provide comic relief. Since many of Ford's films were situated in rural or country settings, his comedy was often provided by rustic jesters played by such actors as Francis Ford, Andy Devine, Stepin Fetchit, Si Jenks, Charlie Grapewin, and Hank Worden. In his military films and rare urban stories,

Ford utilized the talents of a variety of other character and bit actors but few could play the thick-headed fool and foil in these movies like Hymer. Even when he is playing tough like his Big Shot in *Born Restless*, he is funny. In *Up the River*, his Dannemora Dan is the perfect sucker for Spencer Tracy's strong protagonist, St. Louis; while his Rocky Haggerty in *Submarine Patrol* is simply ridiculous when he chains his taxi to a pole by the bar.

## Roger Imhof

Roger Imhof (1875-1958) appeared in four Ford productions: *Judge Priest* (1934) as Billy Gaynor; *Steamboat Round the Bend* (1935) Breck's pappy; *Drums Along the Mohawk* (1939) as Gen.

Nicholas Herkimer; *The Grapes of Wrath* (1940) as Thomas.

Imhof was born Frederick Roger Imhoff in Rock Island, Illinois. He began his career in entertainment as a circus clown and then turned to vaudeville. At the turn of the century, he dropped one of the F's from his name and teamed first with Charles Osborne in a comical acrobatics act, and then with Hugh Conn and Imhof's future wife, Marcel Corinne. After several setbacks while attempting to get into silent films, Imhof became a busy Hollywood character actor in talkies during the 1930s and 1940s, making over fifty movies.

Roger Imhof

Imhof's most recognizable role for John Ford was General Nicholas Herkimer, the Revolutionary War leader of the colonial militia in *Drums Along the Mohawk*. Imhof's Herkimer, who defeated the British and their Tory and Indian allies at the Battle of Oriskany in upstate New York in 1777, has a courageous death scene, but the general's leadership, humor, and humanity during the militia's training is equally noteworthy.

## Si Jenks

Si Jenks (1876-1970) appeared in six Ford productions: *The Village Blacksmith* (1922) as Elmer; *Pilgrimage* (1933) as the station agent, Jimmy Gish; *Doctor Bull* (1933) as Janet's farmhand, Gaylord; *Steamboat Round the Bend* (1935) farmer at demonstrations; *Stagecoach* (1939) bartender; *Drums Along the Mohawk* (1939) as Jacob Small.

Si Jenks

Jenks was born Howard Jenkins in Norristown, Pennsylvania and spent his youth in circuses and vaudeville shows. He had a few small parts in silent movies in the early 1920s (including Ford's *The Village Blacksmith*), but it was not until the 1930s that he began a successful career playing bewhiskered old codgers in over 200 westerns and rural films. One small but notable non-Ford bit was the astonished rustic in Cary Grant's *Topper* (1937) who, along with a friend, (Doodles Weaver), sees Grant's ghost character disappear as he fixes a flat.

Jenks' most noticeable role for John Ford was his Jacob Small in *Drums Along the Mohawk*. Small's best scene occurs when he comes to the widow McKlennan's (Edna May Oliver) door to bring her to the safety of the fort. His "old rooster" is hilarious, especially when he flirts with the widow with twinkling eyes, informs her that he has saved a choice corner shed for her, and, especially, when he gazes around searching for someplace to spit.

## Ben Johnson

Ben Johnson (1918-1996) appeared in six Ford productions: *Fort Apache* (1948) bit; *3 Godfathers* (1948) posse member; *She Wore a Yellow Ribbon* (1949) as Sgt. Tyree; *Wagon Master* (1950) as Travis Blue; *Rio Grande* (1950) as Trooper Travis Tyree; *Cheyenne Autumn* (1964) as Trooper Plumtree.

Johnson was born near Pawhuska, Oklahoma and worked as a cowboy, ranch hand, and a rodeo performer in his youth. He and his father were both world champion steer ropers. He was always good with horses and in 1940, director Howard Hughes hired him to take a herd of horses to California. Johnson soon found work in the movie business as a horse wrangler, stuntman, and double in Hollywood westerns. John Ford noticed his riding and stunting in *Fort Apache*, and soon Johnson had featured roles in Ford's westerns. He also starred in *Mighty Joe Young* (1949), a film Ford nominally produced.

Ben Johnson won an Academy Award for Best Supporting Actor for his role as Sam the Lion in *The Last Picture Show* (1971), and acted in such notable non-Ford westerns as *Shane* (1953), *One-Eyed Jacks* (1961), *Major Dundee* (1965), *Hang 'Em High* (1968), *Will Penny* (1968), *The Wild Bunch* (1969), *Bite the Bullet* (1975), and *My Heroes Have Always Been Cowboys* (1991). He had a memorable comic role as Uncle "Black Jack" Traven in the Louis L'Amour television western, *The Shadow Riders* (1982) with Sam Elliott and Tom Selleck.

Ben Johnson had only three significant roles for Ford but each was singular, filled with wonderful Fordian moments and laconic dialogue.

In *She Wore a Yellow Ribbon*, his Sgt. Tyree has several prominent scenes including his explanation early in the film about the Cheyenne dog soldier arrow, his exciting escape from the Indians by jumping his horse over a ravine, and the poignant episode with the dying Confederate general/Private Smith (Rudy Bowman). And then there are Tyree's friendly quips and jibes at Captain Brittles (John Wayne): "That ain't my department" and "I ain't paid for thinking."

Ben Johnson

In *Wagon Master*, Johnson's Travis is a believable and riveting western hero, and his humorous jostling with his partner Sandy (Harry Carey Jr.) and Elder Wiggs (Ward Bond) as well as his romance with Denver (Joanne Dru) are riveting and enjoyable. Travis has two great short lines in the film:

After watching Sandy hide a pistol down the back of his pants, Travis declares,

"Be careful or you'll blow yer brains out."

Later, Travis shoots and kills the villain, Shiloh (Charles Kemper), and Elder Wiggs remarks,

"And I thought you never drew on a man."
Travis softly replies, "That's right, sir. Only on snakes."

*Rio Grande* abounds with delightful Johnson scenes and dialogue. One of the most unforgettable scenes in this western occurs when Travis and Sandy ride their horses "Roman style."

In a conversation that exemplifies the code of the west, Travis explains to Sgt. Quincannon (Victor McLaglen) and the doctor (Chill Wills) why he presently does not want to go to open court and discuss a shooting that would open his newly-wed sister to gossip.

Finally, there is Tyree's favorite saying of the film: "Get 'er done, Reb."

## Noble Johnson

Noble Johnson (1881-1978) appeared in five Ford productions: *The Wallop* (1921) as Espinol; *Wee Willie Winkie* (1937) Sikh

policeman; *Four Men and a Prayer* (1938) native; *Drums Along the Mohawk* (1939) Native American fighting alongside the British and the Tories against the American colonists; *She Wore a Yellow Ribbon* (1949) as Red Shirt.

He was born Noble Mark Johnson in Marshall, Missouri and raised in Colorado Springs, Colorado where his childhood friend was the future actor, Lon Chaney. His father was a horse trainer, and as a young man Noble Johnson worked

Noble Johnson

as a miner and a rancher. He grew to be 6'2" and 225 pounds.

In 1915, Johnson had a bit role in the Vitagraph short, *Mr. Jarr and the Lady Reformer*, starring Harry Davenport (who also directed). The next year, Johnson and his brother George cofounded The Lincoln Motion Picture Company, an all-African-American film production company that was the first to make movies portraying African-Americans as real people rather than caricatures. Their first film project was *The Realization of a Negro's Ambition.* The company lasted until 1921.

During his thirty-five year career as an actor, Johnson appeared in almost 150 films, playing African-Americans, Native Americans, Latinos, and various natives. He had small roles in such silents as Rudolph Valentino's *The Four Horsemen of the Apocalypse* (1921), Cecil B. DeMille's original *The Ten Commandments* (1923), and *The Thief of Bagdad* (1924). He played Uncle Tom in *Topsy and Eva* (1927). In talkies, he played such roles as the harpooner Queequeg in John Barrymore's *Moby Dick* (1930), the Nubian in Boris Karloff's *The Mummy* (1932), and the Zombie in Bob Hope's *The Ghost Busters* (1940). His most famous role was the native tribal leader in *King Kong* (1933).

In *She Wore a Yellow Ribbon*, Johnson had his biggest role for John Ford, the Native American, Red Shirt. This "Other" character is strong enough to directly challenge Captain Brittles (John Wayne), and is a precursor to Ford and Wayne's greatest antagonist, Scar, in *The Searchers.*

## Ed Jones

Ed Jones (1884—?) appeared in thirteen Ford productions: *Cheyenne's Pal* (1917) cowboy; *Wild Women* (1918) as Pelon; *A Woman's Fool* (1918) as "Honey" Wiggin; *By Indian Post* (1919) bit; *Gun Law* (1919) gang member; *The Gun Packer* (1919) as Sandy McLoughlin; *The Last Outlaw* (1919) bit; *The Ace of the Saddle* (1919) bit; *The Big Punch* (1921) bit; *Action* (1921) as Art Smith; *The Iron Horse* (1924) bit; *The Whole Town's Talking* (1935) bit; *Steamboat Round the Bend* (1935) as the New Elijah.

Jones was born Edward Zachariah Jones in Del Rio, Texas. Jones grew up to be an exceptional marksman. Supposedly, he was

Ed Jones

a lawman in the West. Eventually, he drifted to Hollywood and by 1914 was working as a trick marksman, horse wrangler, technical advisor, and stuntman in numerous westerns. Aka Ed "Pardner" Jones, Edgar Jones, "King Fisher" Jones.

Jones was in several early Harry Carey westerns directed by Ford and, according to Ford, was quite a colorful character. In *The Iron Horse* (1924), he's the man who rescues the boy after the boy buries his father. He often livened up the set and the films he was in by shooting real bullets, and smashing whiskey glasses and even smaller items held in an actor's hand.

## Elizabeth "Tiny" Jones

Elizabeth "Tiny" Jones (1875-1952) appeared in four Ford productions: *The Iron Horse* (1924) woman seeking a divorce; *Drums Along the Mohawk* (1939) as Mrs. Reall; *How Green Was My Valley* (1941) as sweet shop lady, Mrs. Tossel; *The Quiet Man* (1952) as maid, Nell.

Jones was born in Cardiff, Wales. Her nickname was due to her diminutive size. There is little known

Elizabeth "Tiny" Jones

about her life prior to her movie career as a bit player. She made 101 films. Her first (*The Iron Horse*) and final (*The Quiet Man*) films were both directed by John Ford. She also had a small role in Ford's *Young Mr. Lincoln*, but it was deleted.

In *How Green Was My Valley*, she had a lovely bit that adds to the dream-like nostalgia of a scene early in the film, with her sweet old lady in a strange dark hat selling Huw (Rodney McDowell) candy.

In a very short but telling vignette in *The Quiet Man*, she barks at Squire Danaher (Victor McLaglen), a man twice her size, as if he were a child, "Wipe your muddy boots," and he immediately, shamefacedly, obeys.

## Fred Kennedy

Fred Kennedy (1909-1958) appeared in eight Ford productions: *She Wore a Yellow Ribbon* (1949) bit; *Wagon Master* (1950) bit; *Rio Grande* (1950) as Heinze; *What Price Glory* (1952) young marine; *The Quiet Man* (1952) rider in horse race; *The Searchers* (1956) bit; *The Last Hurrah* (1958) bit; *The Horse Soldiers* (1959) Union soldier.

Kennedy was born in Ainsworth, Nebraska and was always an excellently coordinated athlete. He grew up loving horses and became one of the best stuntmen in the movie business, specializing in falls.

Fred Kennedy

Ironically, he died from a fall while filming *The Horse Soldiers* for John Ford.

He was an active member of the group of stuntmen Ford loved to have around. His most recognizable role in a Ford film is in

*Rio Grande* where his short, burly soldier named Heinze battles Claude Jarman's trooper, Jefferson Yorke, in their "soldiers' fight."

## J.M. Kerrigan

J.M. Kerrigan (1884-1964) appeared in five Ford productions: *The Lost Patrol* (1934) as Quincannon; *The Informer* (1935) as Terry; *The Prisoner of Shark Island* (1936) as Judge Maiben; *The Plough and the Stars* (1936) as Peter Flynn; *The Long Voyage Home* (1940) as Crimp.

He was born Joseph Michael Kerrigan in Dublin and worked as a reporter on an Irish newspaper until 1907, when he joined

J.M. Kerrigan

the Abbey Players. He acted in Irish plays by William Butler Yeats and Sean O'Casey, and then moved to New York in 1916 to act on Broadway.

Kerrigan moved to Hollywood in 1935 to participate in Ford's *The Informer*, and proceeded to bring to life over 100 character roles during the next three decades, often portraying devious little men out for themselves. In both *The Informer* and *The Long Voyage Home*, his characters are parasitical leeches who befriend their victims and then abandon them. However, in *The Prisoner of Shark Island*, he is a kindly judge who declares to Dr. Mudd (Warner Baxter) on his way to prison, "I won't be the only Yankee who'll be praying with you."

## Anna Lee

Anna Lee (1913-2004) appeared in nine Ford productions: *How Green Was My Valley* (1941) as Bronwen; *Fort Apache* (1948) as Mrs. Emily Collingwood; *The Last Hurrah* (1958) as Gert Minihan; *Gideon of Scotland Yard* (1958) as Mrs. Kate Gideon; *The Horse Soldiers* (1959) as Mrs. Buford; *The Colter Craven Story* episode from television's *Wagon Train* series (1960) as Mrs. Allyris

Anna Lee

Craven; *Two Rode Together* (1961) as Mrs. Malaprop; *The Man Who Shot Liberty Valance* (1962) as Mrs. Prescott; *7 Women* (1966) as Mrs. Russell.

She was born Joanna Boniface Winnifrith in Ightham, England, the daughter of a clergyman who encouraged her desire to act. Her godparents were the British actress Sybil Thorndike, and the writer Arthur Conan Doyle. She studied at the Royal Albert Central School Hall in London and had her film debut with a bit part in the British film, *His Lordship* (1932). Throughout the 1930s, she was busy in England acting on stage and in the movies. She and her first husband, director Robert Stevenson, moved to Hollywood in 1939, where he would eventually helm nineteen Walt Disney movies, including *Mary Poppins* (1964).

Anna Lee's non-Ford roles included Sister Margaretta, a supporter of Maria (Julie Andrews) in *The Sound of Music* (1965), and matriarch Lila Quartermaine in the American television soap opera, *General Hospital*, from 1978 until 2003. Her third husband was novelist Robert Nathan, author of *Portrait of Jenny* and *The Bishop's Wife*.

Anna Lee always was a welcome addition to Ford's masculine company swollen with hard-drinking Irishmen, cowboy stuntmen, and former vaudeville comics. All of her roles with Ford were solid, but three stand out and feature special moments.

Early in *How Green Was My Valley*, the audience and Huw (Roddy McDowall) are introduced to Lee's Bronwen, her most famous role. Bronwen is a delicate, lovely young lady with a radiant smile. Huw, the camera, and the audience immediately fall in love with her.

In *Fort Apache*, the ladies of the fort are watching the regiment ride away to war. Lee's character (Mrs. Emily Collingwood) squints as she searches for a last view of her husband (George O'Brien):

"I can't see him. All I can see is the flags."

In *The Horse Soldiers*, there is a poignant scene when a frantic mother (Lee) begs the commandant of her son's Southern military academy (Basil Ruysdael) to stop her young son from joining in the school's corps' attack on the Union army because she has already lost all of the other males in the family. The commandant agrees but the boy escapes, and, ignoring her pleas, rushes to war.

## Duke R. Lee

Duke R. Lee (1881-1959) appeared in sixteen Ford productions: *The Soul Herder* (1917) bit; *Straight Shooting* (1917) as Thunder Flint; *Hell Bent* (1918) as Cimarron Bill; *The Fighting Brothers* (1919) as Slim; *By Indian Post* (1919) as Peg's father, ranch owner Pa Owens; *The Gun Packer* (1919) as Buck Landers; *The Outcasts of Poker Flat* (1919) bit; *The Ace of the Saddle* (1919) as Sheriff Faulkner; *The Rider of the Law* (1919) as Capt. Saltire; *A Gun Fightin' Gentleman* (1919) as Buck Regan; *Hitchin' Posts* (1920) as Col. Lancy; *Just Pals* (1920) as sheriff; *Judge Priest* (1934) deputy; *The Prisoner of Shark Island* (1936) sergeant; *Stagecoach* (1939) as Lordsburg sheriff; *My Darling Clementine* (1946) townsman.

Duke R. Lee

He was born Duke Regene Lee in Prince Henry County, Virginia, and worked in carnivals, vaudeville, and the Tom Mix Circus before playing an officer in the silent western short, *101 Ranch Film* (that also featured the debut of cowboy star, Buck Jones). During his long career of over thirty years, Lee appeared in over 100 movies, most of them B-westerns. Aka Duke Lee.

Duke R. Lee was an early, active member of John Ford's company. He was a big, imposing, mustached man as can be seen in Ford's first feature, *Straight Shooting*. Lee's character in this silent western, Ford's first feature, was Thunder Flint, a strong-willed western rancher who has no problem ordering the killing of anyone threatening his ambitions. Lee made twelve silent westerns with Ford and then did a few bits in four later Ford sound films. He can be seen as the sheriff of Lordsburg who arrests the banker Gatewood (Berton Churchill) at the end of *Stagecoach*:

> Sheriff: "What's your name, Mister?"
> Gatewood: "My name is Gatewood, Elsworth H. Gatewood."
> Sheriff: "Oh, Gatewood. You didn't think they'd have the telegraph wires fixed, did you?"

**Jennie Lee**

Jennie Lee (1848-1925) appeared in five Ford productions: *Riders of Vengeance* (1919) Harry's mother; *The Rider of the Law* (1919) Jim's mother; *The Big Punch* (1921) Buck's mother; *North of Hudson Bay* (1923) Dane's mother; *Hearts of Oak* (1924) as Grandma Dunnavan.

Jennie Lee

She was born Mary Jane Lee in Sacramento and worked in burlesque and touring revues as a young woman. She was married for many years to actor William Courtright with whom she worked with in D.W. Griffith's *Intolerance* (1916). She was also in Griffith's *Battle of Elderbush Gulch* (1913) and *The Birth of a Nation* (1915) as Mammy (in blackface). Between 1912 and 1924, she acted in over sixty silent movie productions.

By the time she began working with Ford, she was a gray-haired matronly old lady, perfect for playing mothers and grandmothers. Her mother of Tom Mix's character in *North of Hudson Bay* is a kind, maternal woman devoted to her son. In her five roles in Ford's early silent productions, Jennie Lee added experience and maturity to Ford's primarily young and masculine company.

**Fred Libby**

Fred Libby (1915-1997) appeared in seven Ford productions: *My Darling Clementine* (1946) as Phin Clanton; *3 Godfathers* (1948) deputy; *She Wore a Yellow Ribbon* (1949) as Cpl. Krumrein; *When Willie Comes Marching Home* aide; *Wagon Master* (1950) as Reese

Clegg; *What Price Glory* (1952) as Lt. Schmidt; *Sergeant Rutledge* (1960) as Chandler Hubble.

Libby was born in Hopedale, Massachusetts and attended the University of Maine. He was a big, strapping fellow, ideal for westerns. Between 1946 and 1960, he appeared in over thirty motion pictures and television episodes.

Libby played the disreputable sons of villains Old Man Clanton

Fred Libby

(Walter Brennan) and Shiloh Clegg (Charles Kemper) in *My Darling Clementine* and *Wagon Master*, respectively. In the latter, Libby is the Clegg who is whipped to prevent an Indian attack. Libby's biggest role with Ford was his sutler, Chandler Hubble, in *Sergeant Rutledge*, who provides an emotional scene at the conclusion of the trial.

### James Lilburn

James Lilburn (1927-1992) appeared in four Ford productions: *What Price Glory* (1952) young soldier; *The Quiet Man* (1952) as Father Paul; *The Long Gray Line* (1954) as Cadet Thorne; *Cheyenne Autumn* (1964) trooper.

He was born James FitzSimons in Dublin, Ireland, the youngest of six children born to Charles and Marguerita FitzSimons. One of his four sisters was actress Maureen O'Hara and his older brother was actor/producer Charles FitzSimons. After attending Catholic schools, he followed his sister and brother and enrolled in acting courses and eventually became a member of Ireland's national troupe, the Abbey Players. In the early 1950s, he and his

James Lilburn

brother joined their sister, Maureen, in Hollywood where James began his movie career. Aka James Lilburn, James O'Hara, Jim O'Hara, James Fitzsimons.

John Ford suggested FitzSimons change his name to James Lilburn, his mother Marguerita's maiden name. Over the next twenty-five years, Lilburn appeared in small parts in over forty movies and television episodes. Whenever he could, he devoted his spare time to his favorite hobby, racing motorcycles. During the 1950s, he competed in numerous motorcycle races and won Dublin's Leinster 500.

*The Quiet Man* was his first film and afforded him his most memorable role, the young Catholic priest, Father Paul. In the following scene with Father Peter Lonergan (Ward Bond), Lilburn's character plays the perfect straight man to Bond's over-the-top performance after the younger ecclesiastic interrupts the older man's fishing:

Father Paul: "It's a big fight in the town!"
Father Lonergan: "Listen, there's a big fight in this fish right here, too."
Father Paul: "I'd have put a stop to it, but seeing it's..."
Father Lonergan: "You do that, lad. It's your duty."
Father Paul: "But seeing it was Danaher and Sean Thornton..."
Father Lonergan: "WHO?"
Father Paul: "Danaher and Sean Thornton!"

Father Lonergan: "WELL WHY THE DEVIL DIDN'T YOU TELL ME? Oh, you young..." He throws down his fishing rod and the two men run back into town. They abruptly stop behind a gate.

Father Paul: "Father, shouldn't we put a stop to it now?"

Father Lonergan: "Ah, we should, lad, yes, we should, it's our duty!"

## Robert Lowery

Robert Lowery (1913-1971) appeared in six Ford productions: *Four Men and a Prayer* (1938) sailor; *Submarine Patrol (1938)* as radioman, Sparks; *Young Mr. Lincoln* (1939) as juror, Bill Killian; *Drums Along the Mohawk* (1939) as John Weaver; the documentary, *Sex Hygiene* (1942) pool player; the documentary, *December 7th* (1943) as Pvt. Joseph Lockhart.

He was born Robert Larkin Hanks in Kansas City, Missouri. According to Lowery, his father, Roscoe Hanks, claimed he was a direct descendant of Abraham Lincoln's mother, Nancy Hanks. Lowery was an excellent athlete as a youth and played semi-pro baseball and football. After an injury ended his athletic career, Lowery moved to Los Angeles to attempt to get into movies. In 1938, he was signed by 20th Century-Fox and began an acting career that lasted thirty years and encompassed 180 films, television episodes, and stage appearances. Lowery's third wife was actress Jean Parker who co-starred with Katharine Hepburn and Joan Bennett in *Little Woman* (1933) and

Robert Lowery

85

with Laurel and Hardy in *Flying Deuces* (1939). Aka Bob Lowery, Bob Lowry, Robert Lowry.

His most famous non-Ford characters were Big Tim Champion in the 1956-57 television series *Circus Boy* with Mickey Dolenz, and the political hack, Cuthbert H. Humphrey, in John Wayne's *McLintock!* (1963). He was no relation to the Robert Lowry who wrote one of Ford's favorite hymns, "Shall We Gather at the River."

Robert Lowery had small but recognizable roles in *Young Mr. Lincoln* and *Drums Along the Mohawk*. In the latter, his John Weaver is a loyal and dependable friend and neighbor to Henry Fonda's Gil Martin.

### Cliff Lyons

Cliff Lyons (1901-1974) appeared in fourteen Ford productions: *Fort Apache* (1948) bit; *3 Godfathers* (1948) guard at Mojave tanks; *She Wore a Yellow Ribbon* (1949) as Trooper Cliff;

*Wagon Master* (1950) marshal of Crystal City; *Rio Grande* (1950) cavalryman; *The Searchers* (1956) as Col. Greenhill; *The Wings of Eagles* (1957) bit; *The Horse Soldiers* (1959) bit; *Sergeant Rutledge* (1960) as Sam Beecher; *The Colter Craven Story* episode from television's *Wagon Train* series (1960) as Creel Weatherby; *Two Rode Together* (1961) as William McCandless;

Cliff Lyons

*Donovan's Reef* (1963) Australian navy officer; *Cheyenne Autumn* (1964) bit; *7 Women* (1966) bit.

Lyons was born in Madison, South Dakota, the son of a veterinarian. He grew up on a farm with two brothers and many horses, and soon became an expert horseman. After his father died in 1921, he toured the rodeo circuit with his uncle. By 1924, he was in California working in silent westerns as a stuntman, double, a bit player, and, eventually, as Cliff "Tex" Lyons in a series of low-budget oaters at the end of the silent era.

Lyons was never comfortable doing dialogue in front of the camera, and throughout the 1930s and 1940s he focused on doubling for various cowboy movie stars, playing heavies and doing stuntwork. He soon built up an excellent reputation as a stunt coordinator and second unit director. Many compared his work with the acknowledged master of stunts, Yakima Canutt. It was Lyons who developed an alternative to the dangerous "Running W" tripping wires that caused horses to abruptly fall, by training them to tumble on cue.

Cliff Lyons worked on fourteen Ford films. He was the cowboy riding Harry Carey's horse Sonny in the memorial dedication to Carey at the beginning of *3 Godfathers*. Although his major responsibility with Ford was coordinating stunts, he continued to do spectacular stunts himself and occasionally spoke some gruff dialogue on camera. In *Rio Grande*, when the wagons are rushing away from the Indian attack, it is Lyons who jumps off his horse onto Maureen O'Hara's covered wagon. In *Wagon Master*, he is the angry and sour sheriff of Crystal City forced to deal with the Clegg outlaws, a traveling medicine show, horse traders, and Mormons. In *The Searchers*, he is the army colonel who compliments his young lieutenant son (Patrick Wayne) and Texas Ranger Captain Sam Clayton (Ward Bond) for their work in defeating the Comanches and then ruefully asks Clayton about his buttocks wound:

"You wounded? Bullet? An arrow?" (Bond is reluctant to tell him that it was the colonel's son's saber that did the dirty deed).

## Sean McClory

Sean McClory (1924-2003) appeared in Ford four productions: *What Price Glory* (1952) as Lt. Austin; *The Quiet Man* as Owen Glynn; *The Long Gray Line* as Dinny Maher; *Cheyenne Autumn* (1964) as Dr. O'Carberry.

Sean McClory

He was born Sean Joseph McClory in Dublin, Ireland, but spent his childhood in Galway. The son of an architect and a model, he decided early in life that he wanted to become a leading actor for Dublin's renowned Abbey Theater, a goal he achieved while he was still in his twenties. After World War II, he decided to switch from theater to films. In 1947, he moved to California and that year played an Irish cop in two Dick Tracy productions, *Dick Tracy's Dilemma* and *Dick Tracy Meets Gruesome*. Between 1947 and 1987, he had roles in over 100 films and television episodes. His characters demonstrated substantial range. They could be decent individuals like the co-pilot, Frank Lovett, in John Wayne's *Island in the Sky*; or the shady archaeologist, Jefferson, in Glenn Ford's *Plunder of the Sun* (1953). One of his final roles was in John Huston's version of James Joyce's short story, *The Dead* (1987), in which McClory's character, Mr. Grace, reads aloud the medieval Irish poem, "Young Donal." Aka Sean McGlory, Shawn McGlory.

Sean McClory's four roles for Ford were small but noticeable. In *The Long Gray Line*, he played Tyrone Power's character's younger hedonistic brother just arrived in America from Ireland; in *What Price Glory* and *Cheyenne Autumn*, his Lt. Austin and Dr.

O'Carberry are pictured as far more mature professionals. In his best Fordian character, the I.R.A. villager Owen Glyn in *The Quiet Man*, McClory projects a zest for living and an innate curiosity, especially when he and his buddy, Charles Fitzsimons' Hugh Forbes, attempt to figure out what a sleeping bag is.

## J. Farrell MacDonald

J. Farrell MacDonald (1875-1952) appeared in twenty-six Ford productions: *Roped* (1919) butler; *A Fight for Love* (1919) priest; *Riders of Vengeance* (1919) as Buell; *The Outcasts of Poker Flat* (1919) bit; *Marked Men* (1919) as Tom Placer McGraw; *Hitchin' Posts* (1920) as Joe Alabam; *The Freeze-Out* (1921) as Bobtail McGuire; *The Wallop* (1921) as Neuces River; *Action* (1922) as Mormon Peters; *The Iron Horse* (1924) as Cpl. Casey; *Lightnin'* (1925) as Judge Lemmuel Townsend; *Kentucky Pride* (1925) as Donovan; *The Fighting Heart* (1925) as Jerry; *Thank You* (1925) as Andy; *The Shamrock Handicap* (1926) as Cornelius Emmet Sarsfield 'Con' O'Shea; *3 Bad Men* (1926) as Mike Costigan; *Riley the Cop* (1928) as James Aloysius Riley; *Strong Boy* (1929) as Angus McGregor; *Men Without Women* (1930) as Costello; *Born Reckless* (1930) as district attorney, J.J. Cardigan; *The Brat* (1931) as Timson; *The Whole Town's Talking* (1935) prison warden; *The Informer* (1935) man in the street;

J. Farrell MacDonald

*Submarine Patrol* (1938) as CWO "Sails" Quincannon; *My Darling Clementine* (1946) as bartender, Mac; *When Willie Comes Marching Home* (1950) as pharmacist, Gilby.

He was born Joseph Farrell MacDonald in Waterbury, Connecticut and as a young man worked in minstrel shows and on stage as a singer before turning to silent films. He made his first movie, the short *The Scarlet Letter*, for Carl Laemmle's Independent Moving Picture Company (IMP) in 1911. By 1917, he had acted in scores of silent pictures and had directed over forty, including the Harold Lloyd comedy, *Over the Fence* (1917), in which Lloyd first wore his famed glasses.

In the late 'teens, MacDonald decided to devote himself to character roles. In a career that lasted forty years, he acted in over 300 motion pictures. He was an active member of director Preston Sturges' company. MacDonald played various types of characters for both of his companies, but shined in his roles as tough but affable Irish rascals.

MacDonald began working with Ford playing the pivotal role of the butler in the 1919 Harry Carey western, *Roped*. He had significant roles in Ford's two silent western epics, *The Iron Horse* as Corporal Casey and *Three Bad Men* as the bank robber Mike Costigan. With Ford, he had many parts as hard-drinking Irishmen, giving him the opportunity to quizzically raise his bushy eyebrows, as he did repeatedly in *Kentucky Pride* and *The Shamrock Handicap*. He even got to play the comic title role in the farce, *Riley the Cop*.

In *Three Bad Men*, MacDonald's Costigan is another of John Ford's "good badmen" in the tradition of Harry Carey's Cheyenne Harry but much rougher around the edges. In this motion picture, Ford's last silent western, MacDonald's character and his two partners are precursors to such Fordian outsiders as John Wayne's Ethan Edwards and Tom Doniphon, and to a long line of heroic martyrs.

*In My Darling Clementine*, he has one of the great lines in Ford's films, succinct and to the point:

> Marshal Wyatt Earp (Henry Fonda): "Mac, you ever been in love?"
> Mac: "No, I've been a bartender all me life."

## Jack MacGowran

Jack MacGowran (1918-1973) appeared in three Ford productions: *The Quiet Man* (1952) as Ignatius Feeney; *The Rising of the Moon* (1957) as the poteen (moonshine) maker, Mickey J.; *Young Cassidy* (1965) as Archie Casey.

He was born in Dublin, Ireland and worked for nearly a decade as an insurance assessor before turning to acting and eventually joining the Abbey Theater. Although he made over sixty-five films and television episodes over a twenty-two year span, his  biggest claim to fame were his interpretations of Samuel Beckett, Sean O'Casey, and Shakespeare's characters on stage in New York and London. Aka Jack McGowran.

In 1968, he starred in the "mod" movie *Wonderwall* with a score by George Harrison. He had notable parts as Partridge in *Tom Jones* (1963), the fool in Peter Brooks' interpretation of Shakespeare's King Lear (1971), and Juniper

Jack MacGowran

in *How I Won the War* (1967). His last film role was as the doomed movie director, Burke Dennings, in *The Exorcist* (1973).

Jack MacGowran will always be remembered for his Feeney, Squire Danaher's (Victor McLaglen) resident retainer and tattletale in *The Quiet Man*. Feeney is a little, quick-witted man filled with sizable secrets and vacillating loyalties. The following short quotations characterize is furtive personality:

> Danaher: "Let's have another pint. I'm buying this one."
> Feeney: "High time."
> Danaher: "What's that?"
> Feeney: "I said, that's fine, Squire."

When Sean (John Wayne), Kate (Maureen O'Hara), and most of the villagers appear at the Squire's farm, Feeney slyly announces:

> "I, I think your in-laws are comin' to pay you a visit, Squire darlin'."

During the brawl between Sean and Danaher, Feeney approaches Michaleen Flynn (Barry Fitzgerald), the resident bookmaker:

> Feeney: "A pound on Thornton against the Squire."
> Flynn: "Go away, ye traitor, ya."

## Frank McGrath

Frank McGrath (1903-1967) appeared in nine Ford productions: *They Were Expendable* (1945) bearded sailor; *Fort Apache* (1948) as Cpl. Deric; *3 Godfathers* (1948) bit; *She Wore a Yellow Ribbon* (1949) bugler; *Wagon Master* (1950) posse member; *Rio Grande* (1950) bit; *The Searchers* (1956) bit; *The Wings of Eagles* (1957) bit; *The Colter Craven Story* episode from television's *Wagon Train* series (1960) as cook, Charlie Wooster.

He was born Benjamin Franklin McGrath in Mount City, Missouri and, according to Harry Carey Jr., this "little banty rooster stuntman" was half American Indian and half Irish. McGrath eventually moved to California and by the 1930s, he became one of Hollywood's busiest stuntmen, doing dangerous horse falls, drag scenes, and doubling for many of the cowboy movie stars.

Frank McGrath

McGrath had few lines of dialogue in John Ford's films. However, according to everyone who knew him, he wouldn't shut up off screen. Also, according to Harry Carey Jr. and his fellow stuntmen, McGrath was one of the only people who could get away with talking back to Ford and even called him "One Eye." When Ford would mutter, "I don't know why the hell I put up with you," McGrath would immediately reply, "Go ahead, Boss, send me home. DeMille wants me, anyway."

In 1957, he and fellow stuntman Terry Wilson teamed with Ward Bond on the popular television western series, *Wagon Train*, that ran from 1957 to 1965. McGrath played the cook, Charlie Wooster, a character based on McGrath himself: funny, impulsive and endlessly talkative, energetic, and combative.

Except for his Charlie Wooster character in *Wagon Train*'s *The Colter Craven Story*, all of McGrath's roles for Ford were small bits. But McGrath made the most of them. Watching *She Wore a Yellow Ribbon*, one can't help notice that every time John Wayne's Captain Brittles rides ahead of the column, McGrath's bugler is right behind him, his horse dramatically rearing and McGrath theatrically raising his bugle, attempting to steal the scene.

## Victor McLaglen

Victor McLaglen (1886-1959) appeared in twelve Ford productions: *The Fighting Heart* (1925) as Soapy Williams; *Mother Machree* (1928) as "The Giant of Killenny," Terrance O'Dowd; *Hangman's House* (1928) as Denis Hogan; *Strong Boy* (1929) as Capt. Lash; *The Black Watch* (1929) as Capt. Donald Gordon King; *The Lost Patrol* (1930) as the Sergeant; *The Informer* (1935) as Gypo Nolan; *Wee Willie Winkie* (1937) as Sergeant Donald MacDuff; *Fort Apache* (1948) as Sgt. Festus Mulcahy; *She Wore a Yellow Ribbon* (1949) as Sgt. Quincannon; *Rio Grande* (1950) as Sgt. Timothy Quincannon; *The Quiet Man* (1952) as Squire Red Will Danaher.

McLaglen was not an Irishman; he was born in Tunbridge Wells, Kent, England, the eldest of eight brothers and the son of a Protestant clergyman. As an adventurous young man, the 6'3" McLaglen emigrated to Canada and then to the United States working as laborer, a prospector, a circus and vaudeville performer, and a professional boxer; he allegedly fought heavyweight champion Jack Johnson to a draw. During World War I, he served as captain in the Irish Fusiliers and, for a time, was Provost Marshal of Baghdad. After the war, he resumed his boxing career in England where a movie producer offered him the opportunity to star in the British film *The Call of the Road* (1920). After several years starring in British films, he moved to the United States; his first American film was *The Beloved Brute* (1924).

The next year, McLaglen began working with John Ford playing a bootlegger turned boxing champion in *The Fighting Heart*. Over the next ten years, he made six movies with Ford, portraying physically strong men who must fight against inner or outer obstacles. In 1935, he starred for Ford as Gypo Nolan in *The Informer*, and won the Academy Award for Best Actor. With

Victor McLaglen

Ford's direction and manipulations, McLaglen created a powerful portrayal of a simple man betrayed by greed and self-illusions. Watching Gypo stagger through the foggy streets of Dublin, lost in his guilt over betraying his friend Frankie (Wallace Ford), one can feel the big man's anguish and torment.

McLaglen's last five characters for Ford, his four sergeants and the battling Squire in *The Quiet Man*, each partake in numerous noteworthy Fordian moments and scenes. In *Wee Willie Winkie*, one such scene occurs when Sgt. MacDuff drills Shirley Temple's little soldier-in-training. It is a wonderful study in contrasts: the huge, serious Sergeant dishing out commands to the perky cherub.

In *Fort Apache*, the fort's new commanding officer, Lt. Colonel Thursday (Henry Fonda), has discovered that the Indian agent, Silas Meacham (Grant Withers), is corrupt. He commands his men to open boxes in Meacham's storeroom marked "Bibles" and they discover kegs of whiskey instead:

> Thursday hands a cup to McLaglen's Sgt. Mulcahy: "Sergeant, pour me some scripture."
> Thursday takes a sip and spits it out. "What is this? Brimstone and sulfur?...."
> Meacham: "Perhaps you're not used to frontier whiskey."
> Thursday: "I don't know... I've tasted most everything."
> He turns to Sgt. Mulcahy. "Sergeant, you a judge of whiskey?"

Mulcahy looks around at the other sergeants. "Uh, well, sir, some people say I am and some say I'm not, sir."
Thursday hands him the cup: "Tell me what you make of this."
Mulcahy takes a drink, makes a face at Meacham, and takes another. "Well, uh, it's better than no whiskey at all, sir...."

Minutes later, after Thursday has told the sergeants to "destroy" the contraband whiskey, Mulcahy declares,

"'Destroy it,' he says. Well, boys, we've a man's work ahead of us this day." They pass out cups and begin to drink and devour the stuff.

In *She Wore a Yellow Ribbon*, Quincannon speaks to the troopers before they leave on their mission:

"Now men, I want youse all to pay attention to what I got to say. We'll have women going with us on this trip, so I want you to watch them words. Watch them words!"
A voice from an unknown trooper: "Watch them grammar!"
Quincannon: "Who said that?" He walks up and down ranks and spies a dog lying on the ground.
Quincannon: "Whose dog is this? Whose dog is this?" He pats the dog's head. "Nice dog; Irish setter."

In another scene in *She Wore a Yellow Ribbon*, Sgt. Hochbauer (Michael Dugan) walks into the sutler's bar with five others to arrest the sergeant:

"You're under arrest, Quincannon."

Quincannon: "By whose orders?"

Sgt. Hochbauer: "By order of Capt. Brittles. Are you coming peaceably?"

Quincannon: "Laddie, I've never gone any place peaceably in me life."

He slowly puts down his drink and clobbers Hochbauer.

In *Rio Grande*, Travis (Ben Johnson) and Sandy (Harry Carey Jr.) have just ridden around the parade grounds "Roman style." McLaglen's Sgt. Quincannon is obviously beside himself with joy and admiration.

He mutters, "Boy'o, horsemen!"

Victor McLaglen received an Academy Award nomination for Best Supporting Actor for his acting in *The Quiet Man*, playing the definitive giant bully. His participation in THE classic Hollywood Irish donnybrook is even more impressive when one realizes that he was sixty-five years old when the movie was filmed.

## Molly Malone

Molly Malone (1888-1952) appeared in ten Ford productions: *The Soul Herder* (1917) bit; *Straight Shooting* (1917) as Joan Sims; *A Marked Man* (1917) as Molly Young; *Bucking Broadway* (1917) as Helen Clayton; *The Phantom Riders* (1918) as Molly Grant; *Wild Women* (1918) as the Princess; *Thieves' Gold* (1918) as Alice Norris; *The Scarlet Drop* (1918) as Molly Calvert; *A Woman's Fool* (1918) as Jessamine Buckner; *Sure Fire* (1921) as Marian Hoffman.

Molly Malone

She was born either Edith Greaves or Violet Isabel Malone; sources disagree on her birth name and whether she was born in Wisconsin or Denver, Colorado. She was an attractive brunette who began acting in silent films when she was twenty-nine. She was a versatile actress who did scores of serious westerns and dramas, and also acted in several Roscoe "Fatty" Arbuckle comedies.

Molly Malone was a member of John Ford's company from its beginning. She relished the outdoors, and worked well with Ford, Harry Carey, and the rest of her young colleagues in the cast and crew. Sources disagree whether she had a small role in *Hell Bent* (1918). In *Straight Shooting*, her Joan Sims (with her wild hair) demonstrates a wide range of emotions fluctuating from her early scenes taking great pleasure savoring her small family to her shy, coquettish flirting with Cheyenne Harry (Harry Carey) to her sorrow over her brother's death as she sadly puts his plate back into the cupboard.

### James Marcus

James Marcus (1867-1937) appeared in six Ford productions: *The Iron Horse* (1924) as Judge Jed Haller; *Lightnin'* (1925) as Sheriff Blodgett; *The Fighting Heart* (1925) as Judge Maynard; *Arrowsmith* (1931) as Dr. Vicherson; *Steamboat Round the Bend* (1935) warden/minister; *The Prisoner of Shark Island* (1936) blacksmith.

Marcus was born in New York City. He was a larger-than-life stage actor before venturing into silent films in 1915. During his long career, he appeared in over 100 films between 1915 and 1937, demonstrating great range. In his silent career, he played such diverse characters as the wicked Mr. Bumble in Lon Chaney and Jackie Coogan's *Oliver Twist* (1922) and the excitable Colonel Blood in Laurel and Hardy's *Duck Soup* (1927). He worked in sound films for a decade, and was frequently cast as powerful judges, doctors, and land

James Marcus

barons. Aka J.A. Marcus, James A. Marcus, Jim Marcus.

Marcus's roles with John Ford were usually authoritative figures, often quite comic. It appears that Ford enjoyed using Marcus' commanding persona on and off the screen. During the filming of *The Iron Horse* in Wadsworth, Nevada, Ford had Marcus preside over kangaroo courts and impose fines on those cast and crew members guilty of various infractions.

## Mae Marsh

Mae Marsh (1894-1968) appeared in seventeen Ford productions: *Drums Along the Mohawk* (1939) pioneer woman; *The Grapes of Wrath* (1940) Muley's wife; *How Green Was My Valley* (1941) miner's wife; *My Darling Clementine* (1946) sister of Russell Simpson's character in wagon; *Fort Apache* (1948) as Mrs. Gates; *3 Godfathers* (1948) as Mrs. Perley Sweet; *When Willie Comes Marching Home* (1950) as Mrs. Clara Fettles; *The Quiet Man* (1952) as Father Paul's mother; *The Sun Shines Bright* (1953)

Mae Marsh

woman at the ball; *The Searchers* (1956) dark cloaked woman at the fort next to the deranged woman; *The Wings of Eagles (*1957) as Nurse Crumley; *The Last Hurrah* (1958) mourner at wake; *Sergeant Rutledge* (1960) as Mrs. Nellie Hackett; *The Colter Craven Story* episode from television's *Wagon Train* series (1960) as Mrs. Jesse Grant; *Two Rode Together* (1961) as Hanna Clegg; *Donovan's Reef* (1963) family council member; *Cheyenne Autumn* (1964) bit.

Born Mary Wayne Marsh in Madrid, New Mexico, her family moved to Los Angeles where she was educated at a Hollywood convent. She was discovered by director D.W. Griffith in 1910 and had her greatest roles with him, including "The Little Sister" in *The Birth of a Nation* (1915), the grieving wife in *Intolerance* (1916), and the young, doomed innocent in *The White Rose* (1923).

Beginning in the late 1940s, Ford found her character roles and bit parts. In *3 Godfathers*, she had a memorable scene as Mrs. Perley Sweet, Ward Bond's sheriff's friendly wife, conversing with the three future godfathers (John Wayne, Pedro Armendariz, and Harry Carey Jr.). Twelve years later, she had a small but visible role as one of Billie Burke's character's twittering, gossipy friends at the court martial in *Sergeant Rutledge*. She was also delightful as the nervous mother in *The Quiet Man*, frantically praying as her son, Father Paul (Maureen O'Hara's real-life brother, James Lilburn), participates in the horse race.

## Chris-Pin Martin

Chris-Pin Martin (1893-1953) appeared in four Ford productions: *The Hurricane* (1936) sailor; *Four Men and a Prayer* (1938) sergeant in Marlanda; *Stagecoach* (1939) as way station proprietor, Chris; *The Fugitive* (1947) organ grinder.

He was born Ysabel Ponciana Chris-Pin Martin Piaz in Tucson, Arizona. He usually played rotund comic characters who spoke broken English. He acted as the sidekick in nine of Fox's *Cisco Kid* westerns from 1931 to 1941, supporting first Warner Baxter and then Cesar Romero. Aka Chris Martin, Chris King Martin, Cris Pin Martin, Ethier Crispin Nartini.

Three of his roles with Ford were small, but he had a nice bit in *Stagecoach* as the Mexican proprietor of the way station at Apache Wells. When his Apache wife runs away, Martin has a few humorous Fordian lines:

Chris-Pin Martin

> "Sure I can find another wife, but she take my rifle and my horse... I love her so much. I beat her with a whip and she never get tired... I can find another wife easy, yes, but not a horse like that."

## Louis Mason

Louis Mason (1888-1959) appeared in five Ford productions: *Judge Priest* (1934) as Sheriff Birdsong; *Steamboat Round the Bend* (1935) boat race organizer; *Stagecoach* (1939) as Tonto

Louis Mason

sheriff; *Young Mr. Lincoln* (1939) as court clerk; *The Grapes of Wrath* (1940) migrant father lamenting his children's deaths.

Kentucky-born Louis Mason enjoyed a long stage career before turning to films in the early 1930s. For the next twenty years, Mason played scores of rustics and backwoods preachers, moonshiners, and farmers.

He only worked for Ford in five productions but his role in *The Grapes of Wrath* as a despondent migrant father is one of the most powerful and poignant vignettes in all of John Ford's movies:

> Migrant father: "I tried to tell you folks what it took me a year to fin' out. Took two kids dead, took my wife dead, to show me. But nobody could tell me neither. I can't tell ya about them little fellas layin' in the tent with their bellies swelled out and just skin over their bones. A-shiverin' and a-whinin' like pups. And me a-runnin' around lookin' for work. Not for money, not for wages, just for a cup of flour and a spoon of lard. Then the coroner come. 'Them children died of heart failure,' he said. He put it down in his paper. 'Heart failure!' And their little bellies stuck out like a pig bladder."

## Mike Mazurki

Mike Mazurki (1907-1990) appeared in three Ford productions: *Donovan's Reef* (1963) as Sgt. Monk Menkowicz;

*Cheyenne Autumn* (1964) as Top Sgt. Stanislaw Wichowsky; *7 Women* (1966) as bandit leader Tunga Khan.

He was born Mikhail Mazurkevych in Tarnopol, Galicia, Austria-Hungary. He and his family migrated to the United States when he was six, and he grew up in Cohoes, New York, near Albany. He attended the LaSalle Institute in Troy and graduated from Manhattan College. He grew to be 6'5" and became a professional athlete in basketball, football, and especially wrestling. (In 1965, he co-founded the Cauliflower Alley Club, an association of professional wrestlers; a photograph of Mazurki's ear is the club's logo). After a few bits in 1930s movies, he was "discovered" by director Josef von Sternberg and had a small part in *The Shanghai Gesture* (1941). Three years later, he had his most notable role as the slow-witted giant thug, Moose Malloy, in *Murder, My Sweet* (1944) with Dick Powell. In a career that lasted until 1990, he

Mike Mazurki

made over 150 movie and television appearances, often playing rugged but loyal goons, and was featured in two *Dick Tracy* films (made in 1945 and 1990), forty-five years apart. He also starred in the family-oriented movie, *Challenge to Be Free* (1975).

His two sergeants for Ford are reminiscent of Victor McLaglen's: huge, lumbering men who are leathery tough, yet sentimental and humane. For example, in *Cheyenne Autumn*, Mazurki's sergeant speaks with his captain about the starving Indians they are following:

Sgt. Wichowski: "A Cossack kills Poles just because they're Poles. Like we're trying to kill Indians just because they're Indians."
Capt. Thomas Archer (Richard Widmark): "Come on, Wichowski. You fought Indians before!"
Wichowski: "I fought Indians who wanted to fight me, not just some poor blanket heads trying to go home."

### Donald Meek

Donald Meek (1880-1946) appeared in four Ford productions: *The Whole Town's Talking* (1935) as Hoyt; *The Informer* (1935) as

Donald Meek

Peter Mulligan; *Stagecoach* (1939) as whiskey salesman Peacock; *Young Mr. Lincoln* (1939) as prosecuting attorney John Felder.

Meek was born in Glasgow, Scotland, acted professionally as a child and starred in the play, *The Little Lord Fauntleroy*, in Australia. He came to America in 1894 as part of an acrobat troupe, but a fall from a high wire pushed him back to the stage. He fought in the Spanish American War, acted with several theatrical companies, worked on Broadway, and served in World War I. After the Armistice, he toured India, South Africa, and Australia before returning to Broadway in the mid-1920s.

His film debut was in the silent, *Six Cylinder Love* (1923), which was Thomas Mitchell's first movie. Meek's first talkie was *The Hole in the Wall* (1929) featuring Edward G. Robinson and

Claudette Colbert. Over the next eighteen years, he appeared in over 125 motion pictures, with roles ranging from comic figures, obnoxious intellects, and, of course, timid souls. One of his small but noticeable non-Ford roles was the shifty but paranoid doctor in Errol Flynn's *Dr. Blood* (1935). He was also the hilarious inebriated food taster, Hippenstahl, in *State Fair* (1945).

His four characters for Ford were each quite different. His excitable little man who mistakes Edward G. Robinson's mild-mannered office worker for a vicious killer in *The Whole Town's Talking* has a wonderful scene in which he excitingly jumps up and down in anticipation of collecting his reward. In *The Informer*, his Peter Mulligan, accused by Gypo (Victor McLaglen) of being the informer, provides a poignant interlude with his rambling attempts to prove his innocence. In his most famous Ford role, the quaking whiskey salesman, Peacock, in *Stagecoach*, there is a beautiful scene when Doc (Thomas Mitchell) wipes Peacock's eyes, pats his arm, and has another swig from one of the sample bottles. Finally, in *Young Mr. Lincoln*, Meek's prosecuting attorney is an over-confident egotist capable of giving an overpowering speech, but not having the judgment to be wary of the young Mr. Lincoln.

**Vera Miles**

Vera Miles (1930—) appeared in four Ford productions: *When Willie Comes Marching Home* (1950) girl next to laughing sergeant; *Rookie of the Year* episode from television's *Screen Directors Playhouse* series (1955) as Ruth Dahlberg; *The Searchers* (1956) as Laurie Jorgensen; *The Man Who Shot Liberty Valance* (1962) as Hallie Stoddard.

She was born Vera June Ralston in Boise City, Oklahoma but grew up in Kansas. She was "Miss Kansas" in 1948, and within three years was in Hollywood making movies. In the mid-1950s,

Vera Miles

she attracted the attention of two premier directors, Alfred Hitchcock and John Ford. Hitchcock envisioned her as the successor to Grace Kelly and cast her in the thrillers *The Wrong Man* (1956) with Henry Fonda and *Psycho* (1960) with Janet Leigh. Hitchcock had planned to star her alongside Jimmy Stewart in *Vertigo* in 1958 but her pregnancy cost her the role that eventually went to Kim Novak. Between 1950 and 1995 she made 158 films and television episodes. She was married to three actors, two of them famous: Gordon Scott, who portrayed Tarzan in several movies, and Keith Larsen, who played the title role of *Brave Eagle* in the mid-1950s western series. Since there already was an actress named Vera Ralston when the former "Miss Kansas" began her movie career, she changed her name to Vera Miles, taken from her first husband's last name.

Vera Miles had two major roles for John Ford: the spirited tomboy Laurie Jorgensen in *The Searchers* and Hallie Stoddard, the wife of Jimmy Stewart's character in *The Man Who Shot Liberty Valance.*

In *The Searchers*, she has a telling conversation with Marty Pawley (Jeffrey Hunter):

> Marty: "You know, Laurie, I was just thinking that maybe it's time you and me started going steady, huh?"
> Laurie: "Martin Pawley. You and me's been going steady since we were three years old."

106

Marty: "We have?"

Laurie: "'Bout time you found out about it."

In *The Man Who Shot Liberty Valance*, Miles does an excellent job portraying a complex character. As a young girl, her Hallie is aggressive, passionate, and willing to take risks; the older Hallie may be wiser, but much more careful and withdrawn. She might not have been happier marrying John Wayne's Tom Doniphon, but she would have been far more alive. And this is what haunts her and a perceptive audience.

### Thomas Mitchell

Thomas Mitchell (1892-1962) appeared in three Ford productions: *The Hurricane* (1937) as Dr. Kersaint; *Stagecoach* (1939) as Doc Boone; *The Long Voyage Home* (1940) as Aloysius "Drisk" Driscoll.

He was born in Elizabeth, New Jersey and originally worked as a reporter for the *Elizabeth Daily Journal*. His desire to write continued throughout his life, and he penned or co-penned numerous plays and screenplays during his life, including the storylines to the films *All of Me* (1934) and *Casanova Brown* (1943).

In 1913, he joined the Coburn Players starring Charles Coburn, and in 1916 he acted in his first Broadway play, *Under Sentence*. With one exception (the silent film comedy *Six Cylinder Love* [1923] that featured the movie debut of fellow Ford stock company player,

Thomas Mitchell

Donald Meek), Mitchell focused on the theater over the next two decades. In 1936, he began acting in movies, such as Rosalind Russell's *Craig's Wife,* and soon was one of the most popular character actors in Hollywood. Within the next five years, he had notable roles in Irene Dunne's *Theodora Goes Wild* (1936), Ronald Colman's *Lost Horizon* (1937), *Gone With the Wind* (1939) as Scarlett's father, *Only Angels Have Wings* (1939), *Mr. Smith Goes to Washington* (1939), *The Hunchback of Notre Dame* (1939), and *Our Town* (1940). He later returned to Broadway and acted in over fifty television productions. He was the first actor to win the Big Three Acting Awards: an Oscar (for his role as Doc Boone in Ford's *Stagecoach* [1939]); an Emmy (for his television work in 1953), and a Tony (for his role as Dr. Downer in *Hazel Flagg* [1953], a musical version of Carole Lombard's *Nothing Sacred* [1939]).

Thomas Mitchell also received an Oscar nomination for his role as the alcoholic French doctor and narrator in *The Hurricane.* In this early paradigm of Mitchell's many drunken doctors, the actor does an excellent job of depicting a weak but decent, intelligent man dealing with the horrors and absurdities of life by succumbing to drink.

In *Stagecoach,* Mitchell successfully sculpts the persona of Doc Boone, the alcoholic physician who finds the energy to fight hypocrisy as exemplified by the corrupt banker, Gatewood (Berton Churchill); deliver a baby, and guide Ringo (John Wayne), Dallas (Claire Trevor), and the entire contingent of diverse passenger personalities towards their own particular havens and destinies. According to Hollywood legend, during the filming of *Stagecoach,* when Ford began to bully Mitchell incessantly, the actor retorted, "That's all right, I saw *Mary of Scotland.*" Ford quickly departed from the set and when he returned, he left Thomas Mitchell alone.

Mitchell's third character for Ford was the middle-aged Irish merchant seaman, Driscoll, in *The Long Voyage Home*. "Drisk" is not a drunken doctor but rather a man who gulps down whatever life has to offer. As Ford scholar Janey Place observed about all of these doomed sailors, Driscoll doesn't struggle against his fate, he embraces it.

### Pete Morrison

Pete Morrison (1890-1973) appeared in five Ford productions: *The Fighting Brothers* (1919) as Sheriff Pete Larkin; *By Indian Post* (1919) as ranch foreman Jode McWilliams; *The Rustlers* (1919) as Ben Clayburn; *Gun Law* (1919) as Dick Allen; *The Gun Packer* (1919) as "Pearl Handle" Wiley.

Pete Morrison

He was born George D. Morrison in Denver, Colorado. He rode horses as a very young boy, and drove cattle and sheep as a teenager. He worked as a miner and then for a railroad before meeting early cowboy movie star, Broncho Billy Anderson, who took him to Hollywood in 1910. There Morrison did stunts, worked as a double, had bits and then supporting roles, and was starring in silent westerns by 1918. During the 1920s, he was an extremely popular lead in Universal's *Blue Streak* series of westerns and made such solid productions as *Triple Action* (1925) and *Blue Blazes* (1926). With the arrival of sound, his career declined, and he returned to character and smaller roles before retiring in 1935.

Morrison starred in five of Ford's silent westerns in 1919, working with such early Ford company players as Hoot Gibson, Ed

Jones, Neva Gerber, and Duke R. Lee. In each of these Universal motion pictures, Morrison's character exhibited great riding ability, a strong moral code, supreme courage and confidence, and a sense of humor.

### Alan Mowbray

Alan Mowbray (1896-1969) appeared in three Ford productions: *Mary of Scotland* (1936) as Throckmorton; *My Darling Clementine* (1946) as Granville Thorndyke; *Wagon Master* (1950) as Dr. A. Locksley Hall.

He was born Alfred Ernest Allen in London and worked as an actor on the British stage before traveling to New York in 1923. He toured with a regional stock company for several years before making his Broadway debut in *Sport of Kings* (1926). Throughout the late 1920s, he had limited success in stage plays and decided to move to Hollywood in 1931. There, during the next thirty years, he specialized in pompous aristocratic and butler roles in over 130 motion pictures. Noteworthy non-Ford movie appearances included George Washington in George Arliss's

Alan Mowbray

*Alexander Hamilton* (1931), the snooty butler in *Topper* (1937), and Vivian Leigh's cuckolded husband in *That Hamilton Woman* (1941). He starred in his own television series, *Colonel Humphrey Flack* (1953-54), about a con man who swindled criminals to aid the needy.

In 1933, Mowbray was active in forming the Screen Actors Guild and served as its first vice president. He was a mainstay in celebrity short subjects such as *Screen Snapshots* for Columbia throughout the 1930s and 1940s. He was a member of two legendary drinking clubs, the Lambs Club in New York City and the Masquers Club in Hollywood. His daughter, Patricia, married his friend, actor Douglass Dumbrille, when she was twenty-eight and Dumbrille was sixty-nine.

In *Mary of Scotland*, Mowbray played Throckmorton, the Scottish ambassador to England, who plots with Queen Elizabeth (Florence Eldridge) against Mary (Katherine Hepburn). It is a relatively small role but Mowbray makes the most of it, depicting a haughty and imperious politician to the hilt.

In *My Darling Clementine* and *Wagon Master*, Mowbray's two characters are memorable hams who display their fears as well as their courage when they encounter the West's evil men. The scene in *My Darling Clementine* when Mowbray's drunken thespian attempts to speak Hamlet's soliloquy to an indifferent, savage audience, forgets the lines, and is aided by Doc Holliday (Victor Mature) creates a special Fordian moment; as does the scene towards the end of *Wagon Master* when Mowbray's Granville Thorndyke bravely drives the wagon along a perilous ledge while demeaning himself, "This wagon contains nothing of value, its driver included."

## Mildred Natwick

Mildred Natwick (1905-1994) appeared in four Ford productions: *The Long Voyage Home* (1940) as Freda; *3 Godfathers* (1948) the mother; *She Wore a Yellow Ribbon* (1949) as Abby "Old Iron Pants" Allshard; *The Quiet Man* (1952) as the Widow Sarah Tillane.

Natwick was born in Baltimore and worked with various acting troupes before debuting on Broadway in *Carry Nation* (1932). She focused on strong, often older female character roles,

and she continued in these parts on stage and in the movies beginning in the early 1940s. She was nominated for an Academy Award for Best Supporting Actress for her work in *Barefoot in the Park* (1967) and co-starred with Helen Hayes in the television mystery series "The Snoop Sisters" (1973-1974). She was quite funny as Miss Ivy Gravely in Alfred Hitchcock's black comedy, *The Trouble with Harry* (1955), and will always be remembered for her role

Mildred Natwick

in Danny Kaye's *The Court Jester* (1956) as Griselda, the woman responsible for putting the pellet of poison in the vessel with the pestle.

She had a small but substantial bit in Ford's *The Long Voyage Home* as the sad, guilt-ridden Cockney prostitute Freda who helps J.M. Kerrigan's crook slip John Wayne's Ole a mickey. In *3 Godfathers,* she played one of Ford's revered mothers and has a touching dying scene as she leaves the care of her baby to the three outlaws (John Wayne, Pedro Armendariz, and Harry Carry Jr.). In *She Wore a Yellow Ribbon*, she played the wife of Major Allshard, and has a noteworthy scene helping a wounded soldier (Tom Tyler) who insists she drink the whiskey meant for him.

Mildred Natwick's greatest role for Ford was undoubtedly the Widow Tillane in *The Quiet Man*, a strong but vulnerable woman with a biting tongue. When Squire "Red Will" Danaher (Victor

McLaglen) tells her that he had told other men in the pub that he knew that she would only sell the cottage to him, she angrily replies,

> "So you told him all that, did you?.... Down at the pub I suppose, and in front of all those big ears with pints in their fists and pipes in their mouths."

## George O'Brien

George O'Brien (1899-1985) participated in twelve Ford productions: *The Iron Horse* (1924) as David Brandon; *The Fighting Heart* (1925) as Danny Bolton; *Thank You* (1925) as Kenneth Jamieson; *3 Bad Men* (1926) as Dan O'Malley; *The Blue Eagle* (1926) as George Darcy; *Salute* (1929) as Cadet John Randall; *Seas Beneath* (1931) as Cmdr. Robert Kingsley; the documentary, *December 7th* (1943) as the single voice of the dead servicemen; *Fort Apache* (1948) as Capt. Sam Collingwood; *She Wore a Yellow Ribbon* (1949) as Maj. Mac Allshard; the documentary, *This is Korea!* (1951) narrator; *Cheyenne Autumn* (1964) as Maj. Braden.

George O'Brien

George O'Brien was born in San Francisco, the son of a policeman who later became chief of police in that city. After serving in World War I, O'Brien came to Hollywood to first do stunt work for Tom Mix and then bits. He was an impressive physical specimen, a champion boxer, and a superb athlete. He was nicknamed "The Chest."

John Ford spotted him and cast him in the lead of *The Iron Horse*, and then in several other films including Ford's other silent western epic, *3 Bad Men*. O'Brien also starred in German director F.W. Murnau's classic Academy Award-winning melodrama, *Sunrise* (1927), co-starring Janet Gaynor. Ford and O'Brien shared a close camaraderie throughout the 1920s, but a bitter argument during their 1930-1931 travels throughout the Pacific and Asia ended their friendship; Ford didn't use O'Brien again until *Fort Apache* in 1949.

With the coming of sound, O'Brien's popularity waned and he switched to B-westerns, where he found much success. He left the film industry twice for further Naval service, in World War II and Korea.

O'Brien's two protagonists in *The Iron Horse* and *3 Bad Men* are admirable young men, fairly complex for cowboy heroes, but are bland compared to the trio of Fordian characters who surround him: Corporal Casey (J. Farrell MacDonald), Sergeant Slattery (Francis Powers), and Private Schultz (James Welch) in *The Iron Horse*; Spade Allen (Frank Campeau), Mike Costigan (J. Farrell MacDonald), and Bull Stanley (Tom Santschi) in *3 Bad Men*. Still, O'Brien's two fundamentally moral heroes, with their good looks and subtle sense of humor, hold their own against the scene-stealing trios, misguided love interests, and two casts of thousands.

O'Brien had a strong and multifaceted role as George D'Arcy in *The Blue Eagle*. Competing with Big Tim Ryan (William Russell) for the affections of Rose Cooper (Janet Gaynor), O'Brien gets several opportunities to exhibit his physical prowess (especially in the boxing match) and to demonstrate emotional depth, particularly in his frustration dealing with his character's brother's (Philip Ford) drug addiction.

O'Brien's Capt. Sam Collingwood in *Fort Apache* is an intriguing character. He obviously had some history with his new commandant, Lt. Col. Thursday (Henry Fonda), and all the conversations and interactions between the two men are filled with friction and distrust. Before their final battle with the Indians, Collingwood gets in the last word against his career-long antagonist, "This time you're late, Owen."

## Maureen O'Hara

Maureen O'Hara (born 1920) appeared in five Ford productions: *How Green Was My Valley* (1941) as Angharad; *Rio Grande* (1950) as Mrs. Kathleen Yorke; *The Quiet Man* (1952) as Mary Kate Danaher; *The Long Gray Line* (1955) as Mary O'Donnell; *The Wings of Eagles* (1957) as Min Wead.

She was born Maureen FitzSimons outside of Dublin, Ireland and began acting as a child. Two of her brothers, Charles

Maureen O'Hara

Fitzsimons and James Lilburn, also became actors and eventually worked with John Ford. After work with the Abbey Players, she made her British film debut in 1938 and was soon signed by actor Charles Laughton. She worked with Laughton in two 1939 films, *Jamaica Inn* and *The Hunchback of Notre Dame*, and in 1941 made her first motion picture with John Ford, *How Green Was My Valley*. Throughout the next thirty years, she made a variety of movies including swashbucklers with Errol Flynn, Tyrone Power, and Cornel Wilde; as well as romantic dramas, westerns, comedies, and perhaps her most well-remembered non-Ford film, the holiday classic, *Miracle on 34th Street* (1947). In 1991, after a twenty-year retirement from films, she returned to do the John Candy comedy, *Only the Lonely*.

In her autobiography, *'Tis Herself: A Memoir* (2004), O'Hara pictures John Ford as a vindictive and nasty alcoholic, full of complex emotional conflicts, while at the same time, a gifted artist and director.

She did a memorable job portraying Angharad in *How Green Was My Valley* as the young, idealistic girl who marries the mine owner's son and spends the rest of her life regretting it. The following conversation with her true love, the minister Gruffydd (Walter Pidgeon), is one of the loveliest in Ford's movies:

Angharad: "Look now, you are king in the chapel. But I will be queen in my own kitchen."
Mr. Gruffydd: "You will be queen wherever you walk."
Angharad: "What does that mean?"
Mr. Gruffydd: "... I should not have said it."
Angharad: "Why?"
Mr. Gruffydd: "I have no right to speak to you so." He begins to leave.
Angharad stops him. "Mr. Gruffydd, if the right is mine to give, you have it."

In *The Quiet Man*, she played Mary Kate Danaher, and in this, the definitive role of her career, she portrayed a passionate woman whose pride becomes an obstacle to marriage. When Michaleen Flynn (Barry Fitzgerald) arrives to discuss her dowry, she more than holds her own with Hollywood's greatest scene-stealer:

Michaleen: "I have... I have come."

Mary Kate: "Oh, I can see that. But from whose pub was it?"

Michaleen: "Pub? Pub? You've the face of an angel with the tongue of an adder. I have a good mind to go about me own business and tell Thon Shorton he's better off without ya!"

Mary Kate: "Wait a minute, what was that?"

Michaleen: "Well ye be listenin' then and not interrupting the shockelhorn–the matchmaker... I have come at the request of Thon Shorton..."

Mary Kate: "Sean Thornton."

Michaleen: "Shut up... bachelor and party of the first part, to ask if you, uh–strictly informally, mind you–eh, Mary Kate Danaher, spinster, and party of the second part."

Mary Kate: "Well. Go on. You were sayin'?"

Michaleen: "Actually... me mouth is like a dry crust and the sun is that hot on me pate."

Mary Kate: 'Will you be steppin' into the parlor? The house may belong to my brother, but what's in the parlor belongs to me."

At the beginning of *Rio Grande*, O'Hara's character, Kathleen Yorke, arrives at the fort and sees her husband (John Wayne) for the first time in fifteen years. It is an emotional reunion and as she and her husband walk by Sgt. Quincannon (Victor McLaglen), the sergeant mutters, "Welcome home, darling," and she immediately beams. But then, instantaneously, her tempestuous and self-destructive nature takes over and she has to ruin the moment. Her features harden and she declares, "I see you still have that arsonist with you."

In *The Long Gray Line*, she demonstrated a flair for comedy. In the early scene when her Mary O'Donnell, right off the ship from Ireland, first meets Marty Maher (Tyrone Power), she doesn't utter a word, she just reacts to Marty's antics and does a bonny job of acting with her bonnet.

All of Maureen O'Hara's three Ford films with John Wayne— and their two non-Ford westerns together, *McLintock!* (1963) and *Big Jake* (1971)—involved serious misunderstandings and, at times, separations and divorces. Of these films, *Wings of Eagles* is the darkest. O'Hara's Minnie Wead is initially a vibrant and strong woman similar to Hallie in *The Man Who Shot Liberty Valance*, but after her husband's (John Wayne) injury and his decision to pull away from their family, she gradually begins to fade, as she struggles with loneliness and alcohol.

## Peter Ortiz

Peter Ortiz (1913-1988) appeared in five Ford productions: *She Wore a Yellow Ribbon* (1949) gunrunner; *When Willie Comes Marching Home* (1950) as French resistance fighter, Pierre; *Rio Grande* (1950) as Capt. St. Jacques; *What Price Glory* (1952) French general; *The Wings of Eagles* (1957) as Lt. Charles Dexter

John Ford's stock company is filled with players who led interesting lives before they worked for Ford. No one's was more fascinating than Ortiz's.

He was born Pierre Julien Ortiz in New York City to a French-American father and a Spanish-American mother. He was educated in France at the University of Grenoble. He was a master linguist and spoke ten languages. When he was nineteen, he joined the French Foreign Legion, fought in North Africa as a private and advanced through the ranks to lieutenant. When his five-year tour of duty was over, he went to Hollywood and worked as a technical military advisor. When World War II began, he re-enlisted in the Foreign Legion. In 1940, during the fighting in France, he was captured by the Nazis. He eventually escaped, made his way to America, and enlisted in the U.S. Marines. He spent the war utilizing his mastery

Peter Ortiz

of languages, working for the OSS conducting reconnaissance and sabotage missions behind enemy lines. He was the most highly decorated U.S. Marine member of the OSS. The films *Rue Madeleine* (1947) and *Operation Secret* (1952) are based on his legendary wartime exploits.

After the war, Peter Ortiz returned to Hollywood and began to get small bits in the movies. Ford had been involved with the OSS during World War II, was impressed with Ortiz's war record, and used him in five films. Ortiz has a few brief scenes in *She Wore a Yellow Ribbon* as the gunrunner who, along with Paul Fix and Harry Woods' outlaws, are killed by the Apaches. But his biggest role was Capt. Jacques in *Rio Grande*. The captain is distinguished by two things: his gallantry and his black patch that he borrowed from either Ford himself or John Carradine's villain Caldwell in *Drums Along the Mohawk*.

### Lionel Pape

Lionel Pape (1877-1944) appeared in six Ford productions: *Mary of Scotland* (1936) as Burghley; *The Plough and the Stars*

Lionel Pape

(1936) Englishman; *Wee Willie Winkie* (1937) as Major Allardyce; *Drums Along the Mohawk* (1939) general; *The Long Voyage Home* (1940) as Mr. Clifton; *How Green Was My Valley* (1941) as the mine owner, Evans.

He was born Edward Lionel Pape in Sussex, England and had a busy career in Great Britain as an actor on the stage and in films before arriving in Hollywood. He usually played the upper class British officer or gentleman, complete with a monocle. Two of his more remembered non-Ford characters were Lord Harry Droopy in *The Big Broadcast of 1938* and Babberly in *Charlie's Aunt* (1941).

Lionel Pape's best part with Ford was his befuddled mine owner, Evans, in *How Green Was My Valley.* The scene when the awkward Evans asks the shoeless Mr. Morgan (Donald Crisp) to allow Evans' son (Marten Lamont) to court Morgan's daughter, Angharad (Maureen O'Hara), provides a memorable Fordian moment.

## Vester Pegg

Vester Pegg (1887-1951) appeared in twenty-two Ford movies: *The Soul Herder* (1917) bit; *Cheyenne's Pal* (1917) cowboy; *Straight Shooting* (1917) as Placer Fremont; *The Secret Man* (1917) as Bill; *A Marked Man* (1917) as Kent; *Bucking Broadway* (1917) as Eugene Thornton; *The Phantom Riders* (1918) as The Unknown; *Wild Women* (1918) as Pegg; *Thieves' Gold* (1918) as Curt Simmons; *The Scarlet Drop* (1918) as Marley Calvert; *Hell*

*Bent* (1918) as Jack Thurston; *A Woman's Fool* (1918) as Tommy Lusk; *Bare Fists* (1919) as Lopez; *The Riders of Vengeance* (1919) bit; *The Outcasts of Poker Flat* (1919) bit; *The Ace of the Saddle* (1919) gambler; *The Rider of the Law* (1919) as Nick Kyneton; *3 Bad Men* (1926) henchman who shot Lucas; *Judge Priest* (1934) as Joe Herringer; *Steamboat Round the Bend* (1935) as Mink, pilot of the steamboat *Pride of Paducah*; *The Prisoner of Shark Island* (1936) soldier; *Stagecoach* (1939) as Hank Plummer.

Vester Pegg

Pegg was born Sylvester House Pegg in Appleton City, Missouri. He was always an excellent horseback rider and was an active participant as an actor in the 101 Ranch troupe. He began making silent western shorts in 1912. He played character roles and bits, usually villains, in over 150 motion pictures for over forty years.

Pegg was a member of Ford's initial company and made seventeen films with Ford from 1917 to 1919, usually as an outlaw. After a seven-year break, he had a small part for Ford in 1926 in *3 Bad Men* and then there was another hiatus of eight years before he worked for Ford in four more productions. Placer Fremont in *Straight Shooting* and Ike Plummer in *Stagecoach* are his most recognizable Ford roles. Although they were made twenty-two years apart and one was Ford's first full-length silent feature and the other was one of the first modern westerns, Pegg played similar mustached desperados, cowardly and nervous in each. Ironically, in both gunfight showdowns begun in the city streets, both of Pegg's bad guys are killed by a rifle, not by a six-shooter.

## Steve Pendleton

Steve Pendleton (1908-1984) appeared in seven Ford productions: *Up the River* (1930) as Morris; *Seas Beneath* (1931) as Ens. Richard "Dick" Cabot; *The Whole Town's Talking* (1935) bit; *The Informer* (1935) as Dennis Daly; *The Plough and the Stars* (1936) bit; *The Grapes of Wrath* (1940) gas station attendant in Needles; *Rio Grande* (1950) as Capt. Prescott.

Steve Pendleton

Pendleton was born in New York City and had a long career in 150 films from 1923 to 1960 as a character actor, usually a guy with an attitude. One of his most representative roles was Gordon Wycott, the snooty brother of Bing Crosby's character's fiancée (Judith Barrett) in *The Road to Singapore* (1940). Gordon was the rich young snob who throws some coins at Bob Hope and Bing Crosby's characters after they perform "Captain Custard," resulting in Hope and Crosby's favorite game: patty cake, patty cake, and a terrific brawl. Aka Gaylord Pendleton.

Pendleton's best role in a Ford film was his Captain Prescott in *Rio Grande*. Early in the movie, Prescott sees that there is a woman sitting next to the driver of a supply wagon entering the fort. Prescott mockingly asks the soldier, "Well, Trunket, when did you take upon yourself a wife?" The woman turns out to be the commanding officer Lt. Col. Kirby Yorke's (John Wayne) wife Kathleen (Maureen O'Hara) who immediately puts the captain in his place. When Yorke appears and takes over, the captain camouflages his embarrassment with a quick flourishing salute with his hat.

## Jack Pennick

Jack Pennick (1895-1964) appeared in forty-five Ford productions: *The Blue Eagle* (1926) ship's crewman; *Four Sons* (1928) Joseph's American friend, the ice man; *Hangman's House* (1928) man bringing Dermot to Hogan; *Strong Boy* (1929) baggage handler; *The Black Watch* (1929) 42nd Highlander; *Salute* (1929) football player; *Born Reckless* (1930) sergeant in France; *Airmail* (1932) air postal worker; *Pilgrimage* (1933) soldier; *The World Moves On* (1934) French orderly; *Steamboat Round the Bend* (1935) riverman; *The Plough and the Stars* (1936) British soldier; *The Prisoner of Shark Island* (1936) corporal; *Wee Willie Winkie* (1937) soldier; *Submarine Patrol* (1938) as Bos'un Guns McPeek; *Stagecoach* (1939) Tonto bartender;

*Drums Along the Mohawk* (1939) as Amos Hartman; *Young Mr. Lincoln* (1939) as Big Buck Troop; *The Grapes of Wrath* (1940) camp guard; *The Long Voyage Home* (1940) as Johnny; *Tobacco Road* (1941) deputy sheriff; *How Green Was My Valley* (1941) mine superintendent; *They Were Expendable* (1945) as "Doc"; *My Darling Clementine* (1946) stagecoach driver; *The Fugitive* (1947) bit; *Fort Apache* (1948) as Sgt.

Jack Pennick

Daniel Schattuck; *3 Godfathers* (1948) as train conductor, Luke; *She Wore a Yellow Ribbon* (1949) sergeant major; *When Willie Comes Marching Home* (1950) sergeant; *Rio Grande* (1950) sergeant;

*What Price Glory* (1952) as Ferguson; *The Sun Shines Bright* (1953) as Beaker; *The Long Gray Line* (1955) recruiting sergeant; *Mister Roberts* (1955) Marine sergeant; *The Searchers* (1956) sergeant at fort overlooking former captives; *The Wings of Eagles* (1957) as Joe McGuffey; *The Last Hurrah* (1958) as policeman, Sgt. Rafferty; *The Horse Soldiers* (1959) as Sgt. Maj. Mitch Mitchell; *Sergeant Rutledge* (1960) courtroom sergeant; *The Colter Craven Story* episode from television's *Wagon Train* series (1960) drill sergeant, Tim Molloy; *Two Rode Together* (1961) sergeant; *The Man Who Shot Liberty Valance* (1962) as the bartender, Jack; *How the West Was Won, "The Civil War"* segment (1962) as Cpl. Murphy.

Pennick was born Ronald Jack Pennick in Portland, Oregon. His father was a gold miner and young Jack followed in his father's footsteps before joining the Marines in 1912. Pennick served in China and then in World War I. After the war, he worked as a horse wrangler and extra in Hollywood. Then in the 1920s, he began a fifty-year friendship with John Ford, appearing in every one of Ford's sound films until 1962, and serving under Ford during World War II. (He was responsible for drilling the future members of Ford's Field Photo Unit before their induction). Some sources suggest he played one of the bank robbers in Ford's Buck Jones silent, *Just Pals* (1920). When he wasn't involved in Ford's pictures, Pennick worked as an extra and a technical advisor for other directors. One of his most well-known non-Ford roles was Captain Dan Carroll in John Wayne's *The Fighting Kentuckian* (1949).

Jack Pennick was a big-boned, bucktoothed man who usually played sergeants or toughs in Ford's films. He rarely had speaking parts and when he did, they were brief and terse. His character Doc in *They Were Expendable* was probably his best role as he had the opportunity to act and not just react when he refused to allow John Wayne's character to go on a mission with a serious injury.

There was something comforting in seeing him in the background in all those movies. And, according to many of his fellow members of Ford's company, the big galoot provided Ford with a constant companion to lean on during the bad times.

**Irving Pichel**

Irving Pichel (1891–1954), pronounced "Pitchell," narrated five Ford movies: *How Green Was My Valley* (1941); the documentary, *The Battle of Midway* (1942); the documentary, *December 7th* (1943); *She Wore a Yellow Ribbon* (1949); the documentary, *This is Korea!* (1951).

He was born in Pittsburgh, Pennsylvania and attended Harvard University. Playwright George S. Kaufman was a boyhood friend. Pichel was involved in various regional theaters, including pageants at the Bohemian Club in Monte Rio, California near San Francisco. In 1927, he starred in the title role of Eugene O'Neill's play, *Lazarus Laughed* at the Pasadena Playhouse.

His first film was the 1930 Ruth Chatterton melodrama, *The Right to Love*. As a character actor playing a variety of roles, he appeared in over sixty movies in the 1930s and 1940s; notable parts included Fagan in *Oliver Twist* (1933), Sandor in *Dracula's Daughter*

Irving Pichel

(1936), Apollodorus in *Cleopatra* (1934), and General Carbajal in *Juarez* (1938). He directed thirty-six films between 1932 and 1954, including: *She* (1935), *Hudson's Bay* (1941), *The Pied Piper* (1942), *The Moon is Down* (1943), *A Medal for Benny* (1945), *Mr.*

*Peabody and the Mermaid* (1948), *The Miracle of the Bells* (1948), and two fantasy features co-directed with George Pal–*The Great Rupert* (1950) and *Destination Moon* (1950). He was one of the "Hollywood Nineteen" blacklisted during the Red Scare of the late 1940s and early 1950s. As a result, he chose to leave the country for several years.

Ford scholar Tag Gallagher has declared, "For those of us who think of *How Green Was My Valley* as maybe the 'best' of Ford, Pichel's voice is even more associated with 'Ford' than Wayne or Fonda." Irving Pichel's deep, resonant, and reverent voice provide memorable Fordian moments in the Ford films he narrated:

At the beginning of *How Green Was My Valley*:

"Memory... Strange that the mind will forget so much of what only this moment has passed, and yet hold clear and bright the memory of what happened years ago; of men and women long since dead."

"Everything I ever learned as a small boy came from my father and I never found anything he ever told me to be wrong or worthless."

In *The Battle of Midway*:

"Yes, this really happened."

At the beginning and conclusion to *She Wore a Yellow Ribbon*:

"Custer is dead, and around the bloody guidon of the immortal Seventh Cavalry lie the bodies of 212 officers and men."

126

"So Nathan Brittles, ex-captain of cavalry U.S.A., started westward for the new settlements in California; westward toward the setting sun, which is the end of the trail for all old men. But the army hadn't finished with Nathan Brittles and it sent a galloper after him. THAT was Sgt. Tyree's department."

*This is Korea!*'s closing narration:

"Ask any of these guys what they're fighting for, and they can't put it into words. Maybe it's just pure cussedness and pride in the Marine Corps. A job to do—and duty."

## Denver Pyle

Denver Pyle (1920—1997) appeared in three Ford productions: *The Horse Soldiers* (1959) as Jackie Jo; *The Man Who Shot Liberty Valance* (1962) as Amos Carruthers; *Cheyenne Autumn* (1964) as Senator Henry.

He was born Denver Dell Pyle in Bethune, Colorado. His cousin was Ernie Pyle, the famous World War II correspondent. He grew up on a farm and after high school, dropped out of college to play drums in a band. After service in the Merchant Marines during World War II, he worked in various theatrical troupes and trained with Maria Ouspenskaya. His first film was the Rosalind Russell melodrama,

Denver Pyle

*The Guilt of Janet Ames* (1947), in which he played a masher. Over the next fifty years, he acted in over 250 movies and television productions. Throughout the 1950s and 1960s, the prematurely white-haired Denver played scores of western and rural characters, usually villains or sidekicks. He is probably best known for his Texas Ranger Frank Hamer in *Bonnie and Clyde* (1967) and his Uncle Jesse Duke in the television series, *The Dukes of Hazzard* (1979-1985).

Denver Pyle's roles in his three Ford films were small but memorable. For example, his hillbilly scoundrel who, along with his partner played by Strother Martin, kidnaps the aged sheriff (Russell Simpson) in *The Horse Soldiers*, is a wonderfully likeable rogue. But it is Pyle's anecdotes of John Ford's directional style in Scott Eyman's *Print the Legend: The Life and Times of John Ford* that are Denver Pyle's most significant Fordian legacy. For example, Pyle recalled, "If you had a line and there was one word that was key, he'd walk by and mumble that word. You were supposed to be talented and capable enough to know what he was trying to tell you."

### John Qualen

John Qualen (1899-1987) appeared in nine Ford productions: *Arrowsmith* (1931) as Henry Novak; *The Grapes of Wrath* (1940) as Muley Graves; *The Long Voyage Home* (1940) as Axel Swanson; *The Fugitive* (1947) refugee doctor; *The Searchers* (1956) as Lars Jorgensen; *Two Rode Together* (1961) as Ole Knudsen; *The Man Who Shot Liberty Valance* (1962) as Peter Ericson; *Donovan's Reef* (1963) deckhand who yells, "Man overboard!"; *Cheyenne Autumn* (1964) as Svenson.

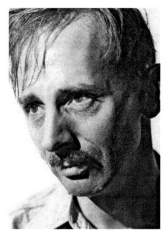

John Qualen

He was born Johan Mandt Kvalen in Vancouver, British Columbia, Canada, the son of a Norwegian minister. As a child, his family moved to Elgin, Illinois, where he grew up. He was a talented musician and played the piano, saxophone, and flute. He attended Northwestern University where he began his acting career. He spent the 1920s traveling with various theatrical troupes, honing his acting skills. In 1929, he played the Swedish janitor in Elmer Rice's Broadway play, *Street Scene,* and repeated the role in Hollywood two years later. That same year, 1931, he worked with John Ford for the first time. Well-remembered non-Ford roles include the confused escaped murderer, Earl Williams, in Cary Grant and Rosalind Russell's *His Girl Friday* (1940); the jewelry-selling resistance fighter Berger in *Casablanca* (1942); the burgomaster in Danny Kaye's *Hans Christian Andersen* (1952), and the merchant who befriends Elizabeth Hartman's blind girl in *Patch of Blue* (1965).

From the early 1930s to the early 1960s, John Qualen had numerous memorable characters in Ford's productions. But of all John Qualen's movie roles for John Ford, one stands out: his Muley in *The Grapes of Wrath.* Muley's famous rant is still as poignant today as it was was over seventy years ago:

"There ain't nobody gonna push me off my land! My grandpa took up this land seventy years ago, my pa was born here, we were all born on it. And some of us was killed on it... and some of us died on it. That's what make it our'n, bein' born on it,... and workin' on it... and dyin' on it! And not no piece of paper with the writin' on it!"

## Chuck Roberson

Chuck Roberson (1919-1988) appeared in eleven Ford productions: *Rio Grande* (1950) officer/Indian who shot arrow wounding Yorke; *The Searchers* (1956) Texas Ranger at wedding; *The Wings of Eagles* (1957) officer; *Sergeant Rutledge* (1960) court martial board member; *The Colter Craven Story* episode from television's *Wagon Train* series (1960) as Junior; *Two Rode Together* (1961) Comanche; *The Man Who Shot Liberty Valance* (1962) henchman; *How the West Was Won, "The Civil War" segment* (1962) officer; *Donovan's Reef* (1963) as Festus; *Cheyenne Autumn* (1964) as Texas trail boss, Jesse; *7 Women* (1966) bit.

Charles Hugh Roberson was born in Shannon Clay County, Texas on a cattle ranch and spent his childhood there and on another

Chuck Roberson

ranch in Roswell, New Mexico. As a youth, he demonstrated an affinity for horseback riding and training horses. After working as a cowboy and an oilfield roughneck, he moved to Los Angeles where he got a job as a policeman guarding the gate at MGM. World War II intervened, but after almost four years of service in the Army, Roberson returned to California where he met the stuntman, Fred Kennedy. Kennedy helped him find work as a horse wrangler and an extra in westerns. Soon he was doubling for various actors and in 1949, in the film *The Fighting Kentuckian*, he began thirty years of doubling for John Wayne. Over the next three decades, Roberson doubled for many of the movie cowboy heroes, became one of the most respected stunt coordinators, and occasionally acted in small parts. One of his most noticeable roles was in *McLintock!* (1963), where he played Sheriff Jeff Lord, the lucky man who ended up with Yvonne DeCarlo's widow, Mrs. Louise Warren.

Ford relished working with Roberson and always called him "Bad Chuck" (as opposed to "Good Chuck," Chuck Hayward). Ford enjoyed watching Roberson and his horse Cocaine take thrilling falls and used the two of them repeatedly in countless cavalry and Indian battles. Ford also reveled in casting Roberson as both a cowboy and an Indian in the same scene, thus often having Roberson shoot himself. Roberson's 1980 autobiography, *The Fall Guy*, vividly recalls his experiences as an active participant in John Ford's company and describes numerous amusing and earthy incidents involving Ford.

## Will Rogers

Will Rogers (1879-1935) appeared in three Ford productions: *Doctor Bull* (1933) as Dr. George "Doc" Bull; *Judge Priest* (1935) as Judge William "Billy" Pittman Priest; *Steamboat Round the Bend* (1935) as Dr. John Pearly.

Rogers was born William Penn Adair Rogers in Oologah, Indian Territory (now Oklahoma). The 9/32 Cherokee boy grew up on a family ranch, became adept with both a horse and a lasso, and attended the Kemper Military School in Missouri. During the first three decades of the twentieth century, he performed in Wild West shows, fairs and carnivals, vaudeville, the Ziegfield Follies,

Broadway plays, and dozens of silent shorts and features. He had his own syndicated newspaper column, "Slipping the Lariat Over," beginning in 1922; by the early 1930s, Will Rogers had achieved vast national and international fame via newspapers and radio.

The advent of sound in Hollywood provided Rogers with the opportunity to expand his easy-going, folksy image, and he soon

became a major film star. Among his eighteen non-Ford sound movie roles, his radio repairman in *A Connecticut Yankee in King Arthur's Court* (1931), his farmer in *State Fair* (1933), his small town banker in *David Harum* (1934), and his newspaper publisher in *Life Begins at Forty* (1935) are representative of his characters who display his witty, homespun philosophy and unpretentious ideals, gallantry, and

Will Rogers

droll humor. Will Rogers died in an airplane crash with famed aviator, Wiley Post, in 1935 at the peak of Rogers' popularity.

Although John Ford and Will Rogers only made three movies together, these were three significant films for Ford. Rogers' three characters—"Doc" Bull, Billy Priest, and John Pearly—articulate Ford's sense of absurdity, camouflaging incisive observations on the effects of progress and civilization behind wry humor and ornery irreverence. These three memorable Fordian characters are outspoken protagonists willing to combat prevailing public opinion to fight the good fight. They respect tradition and history not for their own sake, but rather to give meaning and justification for basic and traditional values.

Rogers' Fordian iconoclastic characters were sentimental yet realistic, confident but unpretentious. And amid all the comedy, there was a stream of sadness and nostalgia. An exhausted Doctor Bull would state, "You know, some old early settler had the thing about right when he said that most of life is a storm and without a harbor a man is lost."

John Ford relished collaboration when he had respect for his collaborator. Ford and Rogers worked well together; both savored improvisation. Ford was very comfortable giving Rogers all the freedom he needed in order to create meaningful extensions of the Will Rogers' persona. During the first day of filming *Steamboat Round the Bend*, Ford asked Rogers and fellow actor-humorist, Irvin S. Cobb, "Do either of you two gentleman, by any chance, happen to have the faintest idea of what this film is about?" Rogers replied, "I don't for one. Something about a river... Tell you what, John. You sort of generally break the news to us what a sequence is about and I'll think up a line for Cobb to speak and then Cobb'll think up a line for me to speak, and that way there'll be no ill feelings."

### Joe Sawyer

Joe Sawyer (1906-1980) appeared in four Ford productions: *The Whole Town's Talking* (1935) Manion's henchman; *The Informer* (1935) as IRA gunman, Bartley Mulholland; *The Long Voyage Home* (1940) as Davis; *The Grapes of Wrath* (1940) bookkeeper.

He was born Joseph Sauers in Cuelph, Ontario, Canada to German parents. When he was in his twenties, he moved to Los Angeles in the hopes of starting a film career. After gaining experience at the Pasadena Playhouse, he debuted in films in 1931 in *Surrender*, a World War I drama starring Warner Baxter. Although his first three movie characters had the names Muller,

Joe Sawyer

Leroux, and Ivan Ivanovich, the majority of Sawyer's characters in over 200 films were Irish, usually burly cops, gangsters, or army sergeants. It wasn't until later in his career that his talent for comedy was revealed. This he displayed with perhaps his most famous character, Sgt. Aloysius "Biff" O'Hara, in the western television series, *The Adventures of Rin Tin Tin* (1954-59). His first wife was actress Jeane Wood, the daughter of director Sam Wood (*Gone With the Wind* [uncredited]; *Goodbye, Mr. Chips*; *Kitty Foyle*). Aka Joseph Sawyer, Joseph Sauers.

Sawyer's sailor, Davis, in *The Long Voyage Home* demonstrates the advantage of using a dependable character actor in a small role. In a film filled with intense performances by Thomas Mitchell, Barry Fitzgerald, John Qualen, Ian Hunter, and Ward Bond, Davis adds to the story's action, mood, and direction. After he responds to the challenge by Driscoll (Mitchell) to "stop winking and nodding and making a mystery of things," Davis expresses the crew's fears that Smitty is a German spy. When it is shown through Smitty's wife's letters that he is not a spy, the embarrassed Davis partakes of a Fordian moment and wordlessly turns away.

### Arthur Shields

Arthur Shields (1896-1970) appeared in six Ford productions: *The Plough and the Stars* (1936) as Padraic Pearse; *Drums Along the Mohawk* (1939) as Reverend Rosenkrantz; *The Long Voyage Home* (1940) as Donkeyman; *How Green Was My Valley* (1941) as Mr.

Parry; *She Wore a Yellow Ribbon* (1949) as Dr. O'Laughlin; *The Quiet Man* (1952) as Reverend Cyril Playfield.

He was born in Dublin, the younger brother of fellow thespian, Barry Fitzgerald. Before he was twenty, he became one of the renowned actors at the Dublin Abbey Theatre, along with his brother. Shields was a fervent Irish Protestant nationalist and fought in the Easter Uprising of 1916. During the next twenty years, he alternated between working in Ireland and on Broadway. In 1936, he and his brother accepted John Ford's invitation to act in *The Plough and the Stars* and both settled in Hollywood. Shields proceeded to work in almost 100 movies and television episodes.

Arthur Shields

His roles exhibited his great range: he could play sinister villains, comic characters, and trustworthy ministers and mentors.

His work for Ford demonstrated that range. His Mr. Parry in *How Green Was My Valley* is a vile little man insensitive to the pain he causes others, while his Reverend Rosenkrantz in *Drums Along the Mohawk* is the most moral of men; witness his horror at having to kill a man. But it is his boxing aficionado, "Snuffy," the Protestant minister living on a lonely island amid a sea of Catholics in *The Quiet Man*, who is his definitive Fordian character.

**Mickey Simpson**

Mickey Simpson (1913-1985) appeared in seven Ford productions: *My Darling Clementine* (1946) as Sam Clanton; *Fort Apache* (1948) soldier at dance; *She Wore a Yellow Ribbon* (1949) as

Mickey Simpson

the blacksmith, Cpl. Wagner; *When Willie Comes Marching Home* (1950) military policeman; *Wagon Master* (1950) as Jesse Clegg; *What Price Glory* (1952) military policeman; *The Long Gray Line* (1955) NYC policeman.

Simpson was born in Rochester, New York, the eldest of four sons in an Irish family. He grew to be a burly 6'6". After a variety of jobs and traveling the country, he ended up in Los Angeles in the late 1930s. For the next few years, he worked as an extra playing toughs and cops; he may have had a small bit in *Stagecoach*. After World War II service in the U.S. Army, he returned to Hollywood and resumed acting in small parts. Over his career, he acted in over 150 films and television episodes. His most notable role was Sarge, the huge racist, who beats up Rock Hudson's character in the diner toward the end of *Giant* (1955).

Mickey Simpson, along with Fred Libby, played sinister outlaw sons in both *My Darling Clementine* and *Wagon Master*. He was one of the prominent soldiers participating in the impressive NCO's ball in *Fort Apache*. But his most remembered role was the blacksmith soldier, Wagner, in *She Wore a Yellow Ribbon* who, when ordered by John Wayne's Captain Brittles to throw Victor McLaglen's Sergeant Quincannon into the guardhouse for being improperly dressed, thinks twice and brings along his assistant and a sledge hammer.

**Russell Simpson**

Russell Simpson (1880-1959) appeared in ten Ford productions: *The World Moves On* (1934) notary; *Young Mr. Lincoln* (1939) as Woolridge; *Drums Along the Mohawk* (1939) as Dr. Petry; *The Grapes of Wrath* (1940) as Pa Joad; *Tobacco Road* (1941) chief of police; *They Were Expendable* (1945) as "Dad" Knowland; *My Darling Clementine* (1946) as John Simpson; *Wagon Master* (1950) as Adam Perkins; *The Sun Shines Bright* (1953) as Dr. Lewt Lake; *The Horse Soldiers* (1959) as acting sheriff, Henry Goodbody.

Simpson was born in San Francisco and participated in the Yukon gold rush while still a teenager. As a young man, he toured with several acting troupes and eventually acted on Broadway before he was thirty. His film debut was in a bit part in Cecil B. DeMille's *The Virginian* (1914). When the movie was remade in 1923, Simpson was the second lead, the villain, Trampas.

Russell Simpson played scores of beady-eyed, weathered rustics in a career that lasted from 1914 to 1959. Of all his roles with John Ford, his Pa Joad, the beaten-down patriarch of the Joad family in *The Grapes of Wrath*, is the most well-known. However, a pair of shorter

Russell Simpson

appearances in two other Ford films were equally as memorable. In *They Were Expendable*, there is a haunting scene when Simpson's veteran shipbuilder, "Dad" Knowland, awaits the Japanese, alone with his rifle, a jug, and the haunting accordion music of "Red River Valley." In *My Darling Clementine*, Simpson played John Simpson, the new church's deacon who declares he has "read the

Good Book from cover to cover and back again, and I nary found a word against dancin'" and suggests they begin the festivities "by having a dad-blasted good dance!"Then, in one of the great Fordian moments, Simpson displays boyish delight and enthusiasm as he calls out to "make room for our new marshal and his lady fair" and fiddles away to the tune of "Oh, Dem Golden Slippers" along with his companions Old Dad (Francis Ford) and the bartender, Mac (J. Farrell MacDonald).

**Pat Somerset**

Pat Somerset (1897-1974) appeared in nine Ford productions: *Mother Machree* (1928) as Bobby de Puyster; *The Black Watch* (1929) as Black Watch officer, O'Connor; *Men Without Women* (1930) as Lt. Digby; *Born Reckless* (1930) as Maurice/the Duke; *Up the River* (1930) as Beauchamp; *Arrowsmith* (1931) ship's officer; *The Informer* (1935) British officer; *Mary of Scotland* (1936) Mary's majordomo; *Wee Willie Winkie* (1937) officer.

Pat Somerset

He was born in London and served in the British Army during World War I before beginning his film career in England acting in the role of Adam in twelve of the *The Adventures of Eve* silent comedy shorts. In the mid-1920s, he emigrated to America. In Hollywood, he appeared in small roles but found enough work to be one of the charter members of the Screen Actors Guild.

In most of his films with Ford, Somerset played British military roles. His British officer in *The Informer* is only on the screen momentarily, but he gives the impression of quiet competence. This is also true of Somerset's British officer in *Wee Willie Winkie*. Somerset was one of the British actors in this Shirley Temple vehicle whom Ford, the Irish-American, continually teased and taunted over the fact that young Temple learned her lines much faster than any of the veteran English thespians.

## James Stewart

James Stewart (1908-1997) appeared in four Ford productions: *Two Rode Together* (1961) as Marshal Guthrie McCabe; *The Man Who Shot Liberty Valance* (1962) as Ransom Stoddard; *Flashing Spikes* episode from television's *Alcoa Premier* series (1962) as Slim Conway; *Cheyenne Autumn* (1964) as Wyatt Earp.

Stewart was born in Indiana, Pennsylvania and attended Princeton University majoring in architecture. He learned his acting craft working with the University Players troupe in Cape Cod and then on Broadway. He signed with M-G-M in 1935,

James Stewart

the year of his first feature, *The Murder Man*. Within five years, he was one of Hollywood's most well-known movie stars with leading roles in *Mr. Smith Goes to Washington* (1939), *Destry Rides Again* (1939), *The Shop Around the Corner* (1940), and *The Philadelphia Story* (1940) for which he won his Academy Award for Best Actor. After heroic service during World War II, he starred in numerous acclaimed post-war motion pictures including *It's a Wonderful Life* (1946), *Rear Window* (1954), and *Vertigo* (1958). His roles during the 1950s in Alfred Hitchcock's thrillers and Anthony Mann's westerns were far more complex and obsessive than his earlier boy-next-door characters, and prepared him for his work with Ford.

Stewart's four Fordian protagonists can be divided into two types. Stewart's Guthrie McCabe in *Two Rode Together* and Wyatt Earp in *Cheyenne Autumn* are cynical and mercenary lawmen whose moral codes are often camouflaged by their pessimistic realism. In contrast, Stewart's Ranse Stoddard in *The Man Who Shot Liberty Valance* is a determined man, brave in his own way, who believes in the power of books, words, diplomacy, and the intellect, and will fight for that in which he believes. In a telling scene in Stoddard's "school," when Pompey (Woody Strode) apologizes to Stoddard for forgetting the words "all men are created equal" in the Declaration of Independence, Stoddard wryly replies, "That's okay, Pompey, a lot of people forget that part."

Stewart's *Flashing Spikes* former major league baseball player, Slim Conway, based on the American pastime's legendary "Shoeless Joe" Jackson, is another resolute man of dogged determination who will not give in to the jeers and jibes thrust upon him.

### Milburn Stone

Milburn Stone (1904–1980) appeared in three Ford productions: *Young Mr. Lincoln* (1939) as Stephen A. Douglas; *The Sun Shines Bright* (1953) as Horace K. Maydue; *The Long Gray Line* (1955) as Capt. John Pershing.

He was born in Burrton, Kansas, the son of a shopkeeper and the nephew of the comedian, Fred Stone, who originated the Scarecrow role in the 1903 Broadway production of *The Wizard of Oz*. As a young man, Milburn joined a vaudeville troupe and, eventually, sang with the Harry James Orchestra. He joined his uncle in the Broadway play, *The Jayhawker*, in 1934 and the next year moved to Hollywood. Aka Milburne Stone.

Stone's first film role was a bit as a sailor in a drama about newsreels, *Ladies Crave Excitement* (1935). Over the next twenty years, he had roles in over 150 movies and television episodes, usually playing gruff individuals on either side of the law. He gradually progressed from uncredited bit parts to significant character roles. In the

Milburn Stone

1930s, he appeared in the Monogram Pictures' "Tailspin Tommy" adventures, and in the 1940s, *The Master Key* serial as Agent Tom Brant. One of his most noticeable roles at the end of this period was the exasperated Major Wilton J. Ramsey in Charlton Heston's comedy, *The Private War of Major Benson* (1955).

In 1955, he began his signature role of Dr. Galen "Doc" Adams in the television western series, *Gunsmoke*, which ran for twenty years. Doc's tetchy and cantankerous personality resulted in memorable caustic bantering with *Gunsmoke's* regulars, particularly with Dennis Weaver's Chester.

Stone's three roles for Ford are each notable. His Stephen A. Douglas in *Young Mr. Lincoln* is a practical and ambitious politician (and rival for Mary Todd) who is duped by Henry Fonda's young Lincoln and his country ways. His Horace K. Maydew in *The Sun Shines Bright* is far meaner, a man who has little compassion for the sacrifices of the past:

> "It is a great and glorious day for Kentucky, when no longer, no longer, can an empty sleeve or a gimpy

knee serve as a blanket to smother the progress of the twentieth century..."

Stone's Capt. Pershing in *The Long Gray Line* is a tough but human career military man. He is similar to Stone's Douglas since the audience anticipates both men's future deeds and accomplishments.

## Harry Strang

Harry Strang (1892-1972) appeared in ten Ford productions: *Born Reckless* (1930) sergeant; *Seas Beneath* (1930) gunner/drill sergeant; *Airmail* (1932) bus driver with lantern; *The Prisoner of Shark Island* (1936) ship's mate; *Submarine Patrol* (1938) as Seaman Grainger; *The Grapes of Wrath* (1940) as truck driver, Fred; *When Willie Comes Marching Home* (1950) sergeant; *The Wings of Eagles* (1957) bartender; *The Last Hurrah* (1958) as mourner at wake, Harry; *Cheyenne Autumn* (1964) bartender.

Harry Strang

Strang was born in Clifton, Virginia and did a variety of jobs before beginning his acting career with a bit part as a policeman in William Powell's early sound mystery, *The Green Murder Case* (1929). Over the next thirty-five years, Strang worked in over 500 movie and television productions. He usually played small, serious bits as soldiers, clerks, laborers, sentries, or cops, but he also did some Edgar Kennedy and Leon Errol comedies for RKO. He played the sheriff eight times in the *Rin Tin Tin* western television series (1956-1958), but his most famous non-Ford role was the desk clerk who gets clobbered in the face twice by a football in Laurel and Hardy's *The Blockhead* (1938). Aka Harry Strange, Harry R. Strang.

Harry Strang's ten appearances in Ford films were all brief bits, but he had a Fordian moment in *The Grapes of Wrath* when his tough trucker and his buddy are touched by the kindness of the café waitress to two of the Joad children (Shirley Mills and Darryl Hickman), and generously tip her.

## Woody Strode

Woody Strode (1914-1994) appeared in four Ford productions: *Sergeant Rutledge* (1960) as Sgt. Braxton Rutledge; *Two Rode Together* (1961) as Stone Calf; *The Man Who Shot Liberty Valance* (1962) as Pompey; *7 Women* (1966) lean warrior.

Woodrow Wilson Strode was born in Los Angeles and was an exceptional athlete as a youth and at UCLA where he played football with Jackie Robinson. After wrestling and playing football professionally, he began acting in the early 1940s and for the next sixty years kept busy making movies. His most memorable non-Ford roles were the gladiator who fights Spartacus (Kirk Douglas) in *Spartacus* (1960); the crewman who helps rescue Dorothy Malone's character in the ocean liner thriller, *The Last Voyage* (1960), and the soldier of fortune/archer in *The Professionals* (1966).

Some sources maintain that Strode had a bit part in *Stagecoach*

Woody Strode

(1939) but that has never been confirmed. What is known is that beyond Strode's four roles with Ford, he was a loyal and compassionate friend to the director during the dying Ford's last months. He actually moved in with Ford for several weeks toward the end of the director's life.

Strode's two best parts for Ford were the title role in *Sergeant Rutledge* and Pompey in *The Man Who Shot Liberty Valance*. As developed by Ford and Strode, Rutledge is a born leader, a force of nature, and a man of great physical and spiritual strength and courage who is defined by his quiet dignity and his dedication to his men and cavalry unit. The flashbacks of Strode fighting the Indians are particularly stirring.

In *The Man Who Shot Liberty Valance*, Woody Strode's Pompey's strength of character is more subtle than Rutledge's, but he is always there to support his boss, Tom Doniphon (John Wayne), be it with a rifle or a shoulder. Pompey is the epitome of the loyal friend and the true power behind the throne who, due to the prejudiced era he lives in, is forced to be silent and subservient, and suppress the volcano of emotions within.

## Slim Summerville

Slim Summerville (1892-1946) appeared in four Ford films: *Strong Boy* (1929) as Slim; *Airmail* (1932) as "Slim" McCune; *Submarine Patrol* (1938) as the cook, Ellsworth "Spuds" Fickett; *Tobacco Road* (1941) as Henry Peabody.

He was born George Joseph Summerville in Albuquerque, New Mexico. As a youth, he ran away from home and wandered throughout America until his friend, actor Edgar Kennedy, introduced him to comedy director/producer, Mack Sennett. Soon, Summerville was one of Sennett's Keystone Kops in silent shorts and features. The gangly, big-nosed comedian stayed with Sennett for six years, then switched to Fox where he directed numerous comedy shorts during the 1920s. With the advent of sound in the late 1920s, he concentrated on acting, and for the next fifteen years focused on character roles. He also co-starred in a series of comedies with Zasu Pitts and played Hoot Gibson's sidekick in B-westerns.

Slim Summerville

Most of his parts during the 1930s and 1940s were humorous, but occasionally he would venture into drama such as in *All Quiet on the Western Front* (1930). He had small but engaging roles in such non-Ford films as *The Front Page* (1931) and Shirley Temple's *Captain January* (1936) and *Rebecca of Sunnybrook Farm* (1938).

Summerville's four Ford characters were each quite ludicrous. His glum Slim in *Strong Boy* wears a ridiculously plush fur coat in the railway station, while his character in *Airmail* never stops the verbal and sight gags. In *Submarine Patrol*, his lazy cook lives in his own isolated world, apart from the rest of the crew, interacting with them with irrelevant quips and wisecracks. The scene when he "volunteers" by mistake for a hazardous mission is typical Summerville and Ford humor: ironic, funny, but never too subtle. In *Tobacco Road*, his Henry Peabody, with his slow Southern drawl and silly asides, adds to the film's absurdities:

> I do declare it looks like my poor head is gonna split wide open with all these singings and yellings and alleluias."

## Charles Tannen

Charles Tannen (1915-1980) appeared in five Ford films: *Submarine Patrol* (1938) as Kelly; *Young Mr. Lincoln* (1939) as Ninian Edwards; *Drums Along the Mohawk* (1939) as Dr. Robert Johnson; *The Grapes of Wrath* (1940) as Joe; the documentary, *Sex Hygiene* (1941) soldier.

Charles Tannen

He was born Charles David Tannen in New York City, the son of a vaudeville player. He and his older brother, William Tannen, eventually made their way their way to Hollywood where they both had long careers as character actors. Charles Tannen had minor roles in over 225 movies and television episodes. He worked for 20th Century-Fox for most of his career, beginning with the coming of age/ aviation drama, *Educating Father* in 1936. As he grew older, he lost his hair and his characters became harder and harsher. For example, his carnival publicist, Owens, in the 3D thriller, *Gorilla at Large* (1954), is quite devious and hostile.

Tannen's most notable role for Ford was his young, inexperienced doctor, Robert Johnson, in *Drums Along the Mohawk.* Here he gives a brief but emotionally wrenching performance as a frustrated physician unable to save his patient, General Herkimer (Roger Imhof).

## Harry Tenbrook

Henry Tenbrook (1887-1960) appeared in twenty-eight Ford productions: *Thieves' Gold* (1918) as Colonel Betoski; *The*

146

*Blue Eagle* (1926) as ship's stoker, Bascom; *Four Sons* (1928) officer; *Salute* (1929) assistant Navy football coach; *Men Without Women* (1930) as Dutch Winkler; *Born Reckless* (1930) Beretti's henchman; *Seas Beneath* (1931) as Winkler; *Airmail* (1931) airport employee yelling "crash wagon!"; *Pilgrimage* (1933) soldier on train; *The World Moves On* (1934) legionnaire in trench with Dixie; *Judge Priest* (1934) townsman

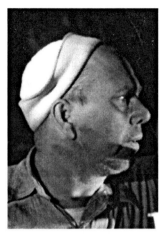

Harry Tenbrook

in bar; *The Whole Town's Talking* (1935) Mannion's lookout gangster; *The Informer* (1935) bit; *Mary of Scotland* (1936) palace guard; *The Plough and the Stars* (1936) bit; *Wee Willie Winkie* (1937) soldier; *Submarine Patrol* (1938) sailor; *Stagecoach* (1939) telegraph operator; *The Grapes of Wrath* (1940) deputy/troublemaker; *The Long Voyage Home* (1940) as Max; *They Were Expendable* (1945) as "Squarehead" Larsen; *Fort Apache* (1948) as Tom O'Feeney; *3 Godfathers* (1948) bartender; *When Willie Comes Marching Home* (1950) as taxi driver, Joe; *The Quiet Man* (1952) as police sergeant, Hanan; *The Long Gray Line* (1955) waiter; *Mister Roberts* (1955) as Cookie; *The Last Hurrah* (1958) caterer at wake.

He was born Henry Olaf Hansen in Oslo, Norway and began his acting career in a 1911 silent short, *The Parson and the Bully* (playing the bully). Over the next fifty years, the hefty, amiable-looking Tenbrook made over 300 motion pictures, usually playing small parts as bartenders, sailors, or gangsters.

Tenbrook made twenty-eight movies with Ford between 1918 and 1958, most of them small bits. Two of his larger roles stand out. In *Men Without Women*, his submariner, Dutch

Winkler, buys a Chinese vase in the Orient for his mother and spends the entire movie attempting to safeguard it for her. In *They Were Expendable*, his cook, "Squarehead" Larsen, repeatedly and affectingly reminisces about his former ship, *The Arizona*, sunk at Pearl Harbor.

## Charles Trowbridge

Charles Trowbridge (1892-1967) appeared in six Ford productions: *Submarine Patrol* (1938) as Admiral Joseph Maitland; the documentary, *Sex Hygiene* (1941) medical officer/narrator; *They Were Expendable* (1945) as Admiral Blackwell; *When Willie Comes Marching Home* (1950) as General Merrill: *The Wings of Eagles* (1957) as Admiral Crown; *The Last Hurrah* (1958) member of Plymouth Club at front door.

He was born Charles Silas Richard Trowbridge in Vera Cruz, Mexico to American parents. He grew up in Napa, California and attended Stanford University, majoring in architecture. His brother was Jack Rockwell, an actor who played scores of lawmen in Columbia and Republic Pictures' B-westerns during the 1920s and 1930s.

After working as an architect as a young man, Trowbridge decided to change careers and became an actor. He worked in San Francisco and throughout the eastern United States in various theatrical troupes

Charles Trowbridge

before arriving on Broadway in *The Marriage Game* in 1913. Although he made some silent shorts during the 'teens, he focused on the theater until 1931 when he went to Hollywood and began a twenty-five year career playing various men of authority.

In his Ford films, Trowbridge played three admirals, a general, a physician, and a member of an exclusive club. (He also played a rector in Ford's *Tobacco Road*, but his scenes were deleted). He will be remembered for two Fordian roles. The first is the army doctor in Ford's graphic training documentary, *Sex Hygiene* (1941), who explicitly describes the characteristics of venereal disease. The second is Admiral Blackwell in *They Were Expendable* who informs Brickley (Robert Montgomery) of the Americans' dire predicament in the Philippines at the outbreak of World War II:

> "Listen, son. You and I are professionals. If the manager says, 'Sacrifice,' we lay down a bunt and let someone else hit the homerun.... Our job is to lay down that sacrifice. That's what we were trained for, and that's what we'll do."

### Harry Tyler

Harry Tyler (1888-1961) appeared in six Ford productions: *Young Mr. Lincoln* (1939) barber; *The Grapes of Wrath* (1940) as the café cook, Bert; *Tobacco Road* (1941) auto dealer; *The Quiet Man* (1952) as pub owner, Pat Cohan; *Rookie of the Year* episode from television's *Screen Directors Playhouse* series (1955) as Mr. White; *The Last Hurrah* (1958) as the elderly retainer, Robert.

Tyler was born in New York City and began his stage career as a singer. For the next twenty years he traveled the country with various theatrical troupes. He and his wife, Gladys Crolius, also toured as a vaudeville comedy team. In 1929, he arrived in Hollywood and began a forty-year career acting in over 350 movie

Harry Tyler

and television productions, usually playing angry-looking old timers.

Harry Tyler had two small but significant roles in Ford films. In *The Grapes of Wrath*, he was Bert, the counter cook, who kindly sells Grandpa Joad (Russell Simpson) a loaf of bread at a discount. Twelve years later, he played Pat Cohan, the pub owner in *The Quiet Man*, and had several memorable lines and scenes, including:

"Ah, what a day for Innisfree. On a day like this, I can say only one thing: 'Gentlemen, the drinks are on the house'!" (The pub patrons suddenly halt their conversations and stare at Cohan).

## Tom Tyler

Tom Tyler (1903-1954) appeared in six Ford productions: *Stagecoach* (1939) as Luke Plummer; *Drums Along the Mohawk* (1939) as Captain Morgan; *The Grapes of Wrath* (1940) deputy who handcuffs Casey; *They Were Expendable* (1945) captain at airport at end of movie; *She Wore a Yellow Ribbon* (1949) as leader of the Paradise River patrol, Cpl. Mike Quayne; *What Price Glory* (1952) as Capt. Davis.

He was born Vincent Makowki in Port Henry, New York. He was raised in Michigan and worked an assortment of physical jobs before becoming an extra and stuntman in Hollywood in the early 1920s. He played the lead in a series of silent westerns for a small studio under the name Bill Burns and then, in 1925, changed his name to Tom Tyler and his studio to FBO. For the next twenty years he was one of the most popular B-western cowboy stars.

During the early 1940s, he starred in two serials, *The Adventures of Captain Marvel* (1941) and *The Phantom* (1943), and also appeared thirteen times as Stony Burke in Republic's *Three Mesquiteers* series. In 1943, Tyler developed a crippling rheumatic condition that limited his mobility, ruined his physical prowess, and markedly aged him.

Tom Tyler

Tom Tyler's most famous role for John Ford was the nervous outlaw Luke Plummer, who dies in the showdown with Ringo (John Wayne) at the climax of *Stagecoach*. But he also portrayed a Fordian hero in *She Wore a Yellow Ribbon* when his Corporal Quayne, the wounded leader of the Paradise River patrol, makes his report to his commanding officer (John Wayne), and later is so gallant and courageous while being operated on in a moving wagon.

### Arthur Walsh

Arthur Walsh (1923-1995) appeared in four Ford productions: *They Were Expendable* (1945) as Seaman Jones; *My Darling Clementine* (1946) hotel clerk; *When Willie Comes Marching Home* (1950) soldier at dance; *The Last Hurrah* (1958) as Frank Skeffington Junior.

Canadian-born Walsh was an excellent dancer and was a member of the chorus line in two of Olson and Johnson's revues, *Hellzapoppin'* and *Sons O' Fun*, during the early 1940s. He began his

Arthur Walsh

film career in Hollywood in *Blonde Fever* (1944) which also featured the debut of Gloria Grahame. Walsh's nickname was "King Cat" Walsh because of his superb dancing ability doing the Lindy and West Coast Swing. He demonstrated this talent in *Two Girls and a Sailor* (1944), dancing with June Allyson to the Harry James song "Young Man with a Horn", and in the *I Love Lucy* episode, *Lucy Has Her Eyes Examined* (1953), appearing as an energetic dance instructor who attempts to teach Lucy how to jitterbug.

Walsh made over thirty movies between 1944 and 1959, usually in minor or bit roles. Several sources declare that, after a hiatus of twenty-nine years, he had a small part as the dishwasher, Manny, in Julia Roberts' *Mystic Pizza* (1988).

Walsh's largest role for Ford was playing the self-indulgent playboy son of Spencer Tracy's politician in *The Last Hurrah*. But equally memorable was his young sailor, Jonesy in *They Were Expendable*, where Walsh participated in a scene that featured one of John Ford's most terse and emotionally wrenching Fordian moments. When "Boats" Mulcahey (Ward Bond) returns from a successful mission against a Japanese carrier, and a group of his buddies (Murray Alper, Sammy Stein, and Harry Tenbrook) begin teasing Mulcahey, Walsh's character, Jones, suddenly notices that a body on a stretcher is being carried off Mulcahey's PT boat:

Jones turns to Mulcahey who replies, "Tompkins."
Jones stares forward, his mouth opened. "How?"

Mulcahey: "Machine gun to the belly. Yes, and we lost the 31 boat too."

## John Wayne

John Wayne (1907-1979) appeared in twenty-four Ford productions: *Mother Machree* (1928) bit; *Four Sons* (1928) officer; *Hangman's House* (1928) spectator at horse race; *The Black Watch* (1929) 42nd Highlander; *Salute* (1929) as Midshipman Bill; *Men Without Women* (1930) radioman on surface ship; *Born Reckless* (1930) bit; *Stagecoach* (1939) as the Ringo Kid; *The Long Voyage Home* (1940) as Olsen; *They Were Expendable* (1945) as Lt. (J.G.) Rusty Ryan; *Fort Apache* (1948) as Capt. Kirby York; *3 Godfathers* (1948) as Robert Marmaduke Hightower; *She Wore a Yellow Ribbon* (1949) as Capt. Nathan Cutting Brittles; *Rio Grande* (1950) as Lt. Col. Kirby Yorke; *The Quiet Man* (1952) as Sean Thornton; *Rookie of the Year* episode from television's *Screen Directors Playhouse* series (1955) as Mike Cronin; *The Searchers* (1956) as Ethan Edwards; *The Wings of Eagles* (1957) as Frank W. "Spig"

John Wayne

Wead; *The Horse Soldiers* (1959) as Col. John Marlowe; *The Colter Craven Story* episode from television's *Wagon Train* series (1960) as Gen. William Tecumseh Sherman; *The Man Who Shot Liberty Valance* (1962) as Tom Doniphon; *How the West Was Won*, "*The Civil War*" segment (1962) as Gen. William Tecumseh Sherman; *Flashing Spikes* episode from television's *Alcoa Premier* series (1962) umpiring sergeant in Korea; *Donovan's Reef* (1963) as Michael Patrick "Guns" Donovan.

John Wayne was born Marion Michael Morrison in Winterset, Iowa, but was raised in California. He went to USC on a football scholarship and worked summers at various movie studios as a laborer, a prop man and, eventually, as an extra for John Ford and others. In 1929, director Raoul Walsh decided to take a gamble and let the young athlete star in the early western talkie, *The Big Trail* (1930). The film was a flop and left the young actor with a new name and few prospects.

Wayne spent most of the next decade working in B-westerns. In 1938, Ford chose Wayne to star as the Ringo Kid in *Stagecoach*. After that picture, Wayne became a major movie star, which continued until his death almost forty years later. Of his 160 plus film credits, he starred in 142. He was nominated for a Best Actor Academy Award for his work in *Sands of Iwo Jima* (1950) and finally won one for *True Grit* (1969). Of his non-Ford roles, Tom Dunson in *Red River* (1948), was one of his finest.

John Wayne had numerous unforgettable Fordian moments. There is his sudden, dramatic appearance in *Stagecoach*; his beautiful initial homecoming scene with his long-absent wife (Maureen O'Hara) in *Rio Grande*; his abrupt lifting up of Debbie (Natalie Wood) at the conclusion of *The Searchers*, and the tense scene when his Tom Doniphon dares Lee Marvin's Liberty Valance to draw on him in *The Man Who Shot Liberty Valance*.

Three of his strongest characters were Capt. Brittles from *She Wore a Yellow Ribbon*, Sean Thornton from *The Quiet Man*, and Ethan Edwards from *The Searchers*. The three following conversations demonstrate Wayne's range as an actor and Ford's resourcefulness in utilizing the actor's skill in different situations (humorous, romantic, and epic):

154

In *She Wore a Yellow Ribbon*, Capt. Brittles and Sgt. Quincannon (Victor McLaglen) are discussing retirement:

> Sgt. Quincannon: "It's an abuse of the taxpayers' money. I told them, sir!"
> Capt. Brittles: "The only tax you ever paid was the whiskey tax."

Early in *The Quiet Man*, Wayne's Sean Thornton romances Mary Kate Danaher (Maureen O'Hara):

> Sean: "Some things a man doesn´t get over so easily."
> Mary Kate: "Like what supposin'?"
> Sean: "Like the sight of a girl coming through the fields, with the sun on her hair. Kneeling in church, with a face like a saint."

In *The Searchers*, Ethan explains to Marty (Jeffrey Hunter) that he has absolutely no intention of ever giving up in his quest to find his kidnapped niece:

> "Injun will chase a thing till he thinks he's chased it enough. Then he quits. Same way when he runs. Seems like he never learns there's such a thing as a critter that'll just keep comin' on. So we'll find 'em in the end, I promise you. We'll find 'em. Just as sure as the turnin' of the earth."

**Patrick Wayne**

Patrick Wayne (born 1939) appeared in ten Ford productions: *Rio Grande* (1950) boy; *The Quiet Man* (1952) boy on wagon at horse race; *The Sun Shines Bright* (1953) cadet; *Rookie of the Year* episode from television's *Screen Directors Playhouse* (1955) as Lyn Goodhue; *The Long Gray Line* (1955) as Abner "Chub" Overton; *Mister Roberts* (1955) as Bookser; *The Searchers* (1956) as Lt.

Patrick Wayne

Greenhill; *Flashing Spikes* episode from television's *Alcoa Premier* series (1962) as Bill Riley; *Donovan's Reef* (1963) Australian navy lieutenant; *Cheyenne Autumn* (1964) as 2nd Lt. Scott.

He was born Patrick John Morrison in Los Angeles, the second son of movie star John Wayne. He graduated from Loyola Marymount University and went on to act in television and in such non-Ford films as *Shenandoah* (1965), *McLintock!* (1963) and *Big Jake* (1971). In 1977, he starred in *Sinbad and the Eye of the Tiger* and *The People That Time Forgot*.

As a youth, he had bits in several John Ford motion pictures, and later had larger roles in Ford's films and in two television productions about baseball. His best role with Ford was his youthful and enthusiastic cavalry officer in *The Searchers* whom John Wayne's character has a good time teasing and who exasperates (and embarrasses) Ward Bond's Texas Ranger captain.

## O.Z. Whitehead

O.Z. Whitehead (1911-1998) appeared in five Ford productions: *The Grapes of Wrath* (1940) as Al Joad; *The Last Hurrah* (1958) as Norman Cass Jr.; *The Horse Soldiers* (1959) as

Otis "Hoppy" Hopkins; *Two Rode Together* (1961) as Lt. Chase; *The Man Who Shot Liberty Valance* (1962) as Herbert Carruthers.

O.Z. Whitehead

He was born Othout Zabriskie Whitehead in New York City, the son of a prosperous and prominent banker, and attended Harvard University. During the 1930s, he appeared in twelve Broadway plays, debuting in *The Lake* (1933), Katharine Hepburn's first leading Broadway role.

His first Hollywood film was the ghost story drama, *The Scoundrel* (1935), starring Noel Coward. Over the next thirty years, he acted in over forty motion picture and television productions. During the 1950s and 1960s, he became a convert to the Baha'i Faith and wrote three books on its teachings.

Whitehead's five Ford characters were each quite different individuals. His Al Joad in *The Grapes of Wrath* is overshadowed by his brother Tom (Henry Fonda), but Al's a plodder who refuses to quit. In *The Last Hurrah*, his Norman Cass Jr. is an idiot. In *The Horse Soldiers*, his Otis Hopkins is a scholarly and compassionate physician's assistant who is unwaveringly loyal to his doctor (William Holden) and to the welfare of his patients. In *Two Rode Together*, his Lt. Chase is a military man schooled to follow orders, while his Herbert Carruthers in *The Man Who Shot Liberty Valance* is a big, lollypop-chewing schoolboy.

## Grant Withers

Grant Withers (1904-1959) appeared in five Ford productions: *Upstream* (1927) as Juan Rodriguez/Jack LaVelle; *My Darling Clementine* (1946) as Ike Clanton; *Fort Apache* (1948) as Silas Meacham; *Rio Grande* (1950) U.S. Marshall; *The Sun Shines Bright* (1953) as Buck Ramsey

He was born Granville G. Withers in Pueblo, Colorado; went to the Kemper Military School in Missouri (the same school Will Rogers attended twenty years prior), and worked for an oil

Grant Withers

company and as a newspaper reporter before arriving in Hollywood in the mid-1920s. For the next ten years, he alternated between starring in films and doing character work. He co-starred several times with Dolores Costello and twice with his second wife, Loretta Young, whom he eloped with when she was seventeen. Ironically, their second picture together was titled *Too Young to Marry* (1931).

Withers played the title role in the *Jungle Jim* serial (1937) and was the aggressive police captain in Boris Karloff's *Mr. Wong* series beginning in 1938. Throughout the 1940s and 1950s, he appeared in numerous supporting roles, usually as villains. He did portray a humorous character alongside Victor McLaglen in Maureen O'Hara's *Lady Godiva of Coventry* (1955). His fifth wife was actress Estelita Rodriguez who played the Mexican spouse of the friendly hotel proprietor (Pedro Gonzalez Gonzalez) in Howard Hawks' *Rio Bravo* (1959).

Grant Withers did a good job playing stupid in his roles as the U.S. Marshall in *Rio Grande* and Buck Ramsey in *The Sun Shines Bright*, but it is his corrupt Indian agent, Silas Meacham in *Fort Apache*, who will be remembered, particularly in the scene in his storeroom when Lt. Col. Owen Thursday (Henry Fonda) discovers his corruption:

"Mr. Meacham, you're a blackguard, a liar, a hypocrite, and a stench in the nostrils of honest men."

**Hank Worden**

Hank Worden (1901-1992) appeared in nine Ford productions: *Stagecoach* (1939) cavalryman; *Fort Apache* (1948) Southern recruit; *3 Godfathers* (1948) as Deputy Curly; *When Willie Comes Marching Home* (1950) marching band leader; *Wagon Master* (1950) as Luke Clegg; *The Searchers* (1956) as Mose Harper; *The Horse Soldiers* (1959) as Deacon Clump; *Sergeant Rutledge* (1960) as Laredo; *The Colter Craven Story* episode from television's *Wagon Train* series (1960) as Hank.

Hank Worden

Worden was born Norton Earl Worden in Rolfe, Iowa and grew up on a ranch in Montana before attending Stanford University and the University of Nevada, majoring in engineering. After failing to become an army pilot, he traveled the rodeo circuit as a bronco rider. In 1931, he and Tex Ritter were seen participating in a rodeo in Madison Square Garden in New York City and were hired to appear in the Broadway play, *Green Grow the Lilacs*, the play from which the musical *Oklahoma!* was derived. Worden went on to make over 200 movies and television shows from the mid-1930s into the 1990s. He worked with John Wayne in seventeen movies; one of his most noticeable non-Ford characters was Parson in *The Alamo* (1960).

Sources disagree whether Worden had a bit part in *The Quiet Man* (1952) as Sean Thornton's (John Wayne) corner man in the boxing scene flashback.

All of Hank Worden's other roles in John Ford's movies pale in comparison to his portrayal of the guileless but canny Mose Harper in *The Searchers*. In such scenes as Mose's gesturing as Ethan Edwards (John Wayne) explains why he shot a dead Indian's eyes out, Mose's declaration prior to an Indian battle ("That which we are about to receive, we thank thee, O Lord."), and his thanks to Mrs. Jorgensen (Olive Carey) ("Grateful to the hospitality of your rocking chair, ma'am."), Old Mose Harper proves to be one of John Ford's most engaging jesters.

## Carleton Young

Carleton Young (1905-1994) appeared in seven Ford productions: *The Last Hurrah* (1958) as Winslow; *The Horse Soldiers* (1959) as Confederate Col. Jonathan Miles; *Sergeant Rutledge* (1960) as prosecuting attorney Captain Shattuck; *The Colter Craven Story* episode from television's *Wagon Train* series (1960) as Dr. Colter Craven; *The Man Who Shot Liberty Valance* (1962) as newspaper editor Maxwell Scott; *Flashing Spikes* episode from television's *Alcoa Premier* series (1962) as Rex Short; *Cheyenne Autumn* (1964) aide to Secretary of the Interior, Carl Schurz (Edward G. Robinson).

He was born Carleton Scott Young in Westfield, New York and appeared on Broadway during the early 1930s in numerous plays, including *Page Pygmalion* and *Yesterday's Orchards*. Young had a deep baritone voice and by the mid-1930s, he had moved to Hollywood and was progressing from bit parts to larger roles. He had a significant role as a drug dealer in *Reefer Madness* (1936), was Dick Tracy's brother

Carleton Young

in *Dick Tracy* (1937), and worked for years at Republic, often in B-westerns and serials. Young worked in films and then television for almost forty years and had almost 250 roles. He is occasionally confused with radio performer and movie actor Carleton G. Young, who co-starred with Esther Williams and Van Johnson in *Thrill of a Romance* (1945). Carleton Young was married for almost fifty years to Noel Toy, famous as an exotic dancer and nicknamed "The Chinese Sally Rand."

In Ford's films, Young gave powerful performances as men of authority with strong convictions and opinions. His Confederate colonel in *The Horse Soldiers* is willing to die for the southern cause while his odious prosecuting attorney at the court martial in *Sergeant Rutledge* will do anything to win the case. But it is his newspaper editor, Maxwell Scott, who is the most well-remembered Fordian character, with his fifteen-word answer to James Stewart's Ransom Stoddard question, "You're not going to use the story, Mr. Scott?"

"No, sir. This is the West, sir. When the legend becomes fact, print the legend."

# One Hundred Twenty-Six John Ford Projects with Participating Stock Company Members

This listing includes 117 of John Ford's theatrical films, five documentaries, and four television productions.

*The Soul Herder* (1917) (Universal): Harry Carey, Duke R. Lee, Vester Pegg, Bill Gettinger/ Bill Steel, Hoot Gibson, Molly Malone.

*Cheyenne's Pal* (1917) (Universal): Harry Carey, Vester Pegg, Bill Gettinger/Bill Steel, Hoot Gibson, Ed Jones.

*Straight Shooting* (1917) (Universal): Harry Carey, Molly Malone, Duke R. Lee, Vester Pegg, Hoot Gibson.

*The Secret Man* (1917) (Universal): Harry Carey, Vester Pegg, Bill Gettinger/Bill Steel, Hoot Gibson

*A Marked Man* (1917) (Universal): Harry Carey, Molly Malone, Vester Pegg, Bill Gettinger/Bill Steel, Hoot Gibson.

*Bucking Broadway* (1917) (Universal): Harry Carey, Molly Malone, Vester Pegg, Bill Gettinger/Bill Steel.

*The Phantom Riders* (1918) (Universal): Harry Carey, Molly Malone, Vester Pegg, Bill Gettinger/Bill Steel.

*Wild Women* (1918) (Universal): Harry Carey, Molly Malone, Vester Pegg, Ed Jones.

*Thieves' Gold* (1918) (Universal): Harry Carey, Molly Malone, Vester Pegg, Harry Tenbrook.

*The Scarlet Drop* (1918) (Universal): Harry Carey, Molly Malone, Vester Pegg.

*Hell Bent* (1918) (Universal): Harry Carey, Neva Gerber, Duke R. Lee, Vester Pegg, Joe Harris.

*A Woman's Fool* (1918) (Universal): Harry Carey, Molly Malone, Ed Jones, Vester Pegg.

*Three Mounted Men* (1918) (Universal): Harry Carey, Neva Gerber, Joe Harris.

*Roped* (1919) (Universal): Harry Carey, Neva Gerber, J. Farrell MacDonald.

*The Fighting Brothers* (1919) (Universal): Pete Morrison, Hoot Gibson, Duke R. Lee.

*A Fight for Love* (1919) (Universal): Harry Carey, Joe Harris, Neva Gerber, J. Farrell MacDonald, Chief John Big Tree.

*By Indian Post* (1919) (Universal): Pete Morrison, Duke R. Lee, Ed Jones, Hoot Gibson.

*The Rustlers* (1919) (Universal): Pete Morrison, Hoot Gibson.

*Bare Fists* (1919) (Universal): Harry Carey, Vester Pegg, Joe Harris.

*Gun Law* (1919) (Universal): Pete Morrison, Hoot Gibson, Ed Jones.

*The Gun Packer* (1919) (Universal): Ed Jones, Pete Morrison, Hoot Gibson, Duke R. Lee.

*Riders of Vengeance* (1919) (Universal): Harry Carey, Joe Harris, J. Farrell MacDonald, Jennie Lee, Vester Pegg.

*The Last Outlaw* (1919) (Universal): Ed Jones.

*The Outcasts of Poker Flat* (1919) (Universal): Harry Carey, Joe Harris, J. Farrell MacDonald, Duke R. Lee, Vester Pegg.

*The Ace of the Saddle* (1919) (Universal): Harry Carey, Joe Harris, Duke R. Lee, Vester Pegg, Ed Jones.

*The Rider of the Law* (1919) (Universal): Harry Carey, Vester Pegg, Joe Harris, Duke R. Lee, Jennie Lee.

*A Gun Fightin' Gentleman* (1919) (Universal-Special): Harry Carey, Duke R. Lee, Joe Harris.

*Marked Men* (1919) (Universal): Harry Carey, J. Farrell MacDonald, Joe Harris.

*Hitchin' Posts* (1920) (Universal): Joe Harris, J. Farrell MacDonald, Duke R. Lee.

*Just Pals* (1920) (Fox): Duke R. Lee.

*The Big Punch* (1921) (Fox): Jennie Lee, Ed Jones,

*The Freeze-Out* (1921) (Universal): Harry Carey, Joe Harris, J. Farrell MacDonald.

*The Wallop* (1921) (Universal): Harry Carey, Joe Harris, J. Farrell MacDonald, Bill Gettinger/Bill Steel, Noble Johnson.

*Desperate Trails* (1921) (Universal): Harry Carey.

*Action* (1921) (Universal): Hoot Gibson, Francis Ford, J. Farrell MacDonald, Ed Jones.

*Sure Fire* (1921) (Universal): Hoot Gibson, Molly Malone, Joe Harris.

*The Village Blacksmith* (1922) (Fox): Francis Ford, Si Jenks.

*The Face on the Bar-Room Floor* (1923) (Fox): Ruth Clifford.

*Three Jumps Ahead* (1923) (Fox): Francis Ford.

*Cameo Kirby* (1923) (Fox): Frank Baker.

*North of Hudson Bay* (1923) (Fox): Jennie Lee, Frank Campeau.

*Hoodman Blind* (1923) (Fox): Frank Campeau.

*The Iron Horse* (1924) (Fox): George O'Brien, James Marcus, J. Farrell MacDonald, Ed Jones, Chief John Big Tree, Dan Borzage, Elizabeth "Tiny" Jones.

*Hearts of Oak* (1924) (Fox): Jennie Lee, Francis Ford, Frank Baker.

*Lightnin'* (1925) (Fox): J. Farrell MacDonald, James Marcus, Brandon Hurst.

*Kentucky Pride* (1925) (Fox): J. Farrell MacDonald.

*The Fighting Heart* (1925) (Fox): George O'Brien, J. Farrell MacDonald, Victor McLaglen, James Marcus, Francis Ford, Frank Baker.

*Thank You* (1925) (Fox): George O'Brien, J. Farrell MacDonald.

*The Shamrock Handicap* (1926) (Fox): J. Farrell MacDonald, Brandon Hurst.

*3 Bad Men* (1926) (Fox): George O'Brien, J. Farrell MacDonald, Frank Campeau, Vester Pegg.

*The Blue Eagle* (1926) (Fox): George O'Brien, Harry Tenbrook, Jack Pennick.

*Upstream* (1927) (Fox): Earle Foxe, Grant Withers, Francis Ford.

*Mother Machree* (1928) (Fox): Victor McLaglen, Pat Somerset, John Wayne.

*Four Sons* (1928) (Fox): Earle Foxe, Jack Pennick, Harry Tenbrook, John Wayne, Frank Baker.

*Hangman's House* (1928) (Fox): Victor McLaglen, John Wayne, Jack Pennick, Earle Foxe, Mary Gordon, Frank Baker.

*Riley the Cop* (1928) (Fox): J. Farrell MacDonald.

*Strong Boy* (1929) (Fox): Victor McLaglen, Slim Summerville, Jack Pennick, J. Farrell MacDonald.

*The Black Watch* (1929) (Fox): Victor McLaglen, Francis Ford, Frank Baker, Jack Pennick, Mary Gordon, Pat Somerset, John Wayne.

*Salute* (1929) (Fox): George O'Brien, Frank Albertson, Stepin Fetchit, Harry Tenbrook, Ward Bond, John Wayne, Ben Hall, Jack Pennick.

*Men Without Women* (1930) (Fox): Frank Albertson, Warren Hymer, J. Farrell MacDonald, Harry Tenbrook, John Wayne, Pat Somerset, Frank Baker.

*Born Reckless* (1930) (Fox): Warren Hymer, Frank Albertson, J. Farrell MacDonald, Jack Pennick, Ward Bond, Robert Homans, Harry Tenbrook, Pat Somerset, John Wayne, Harry Strang.

*Up the River* (1930) (Fox): Warren Hymer, Steve Pendleton, Ward Bond, Pat Somerset.

*Seas Beneath* (1931) (Fox): George O'Brien, Warren Hymer, Harry Tenbrook, Francis Ford, Ben Hall, Steve Pendleton, Harry Strang, Frank Baker.

*The Brat* (1931) (Fox): Frank Albertson, J. Farrell MacDonald, Ward Bond.

*Arrowsmith* (1931) (Goldwyn-United Artists): Ward Bond, Frank Baker, James Marcus, John Qualen, Pat Somerset.

*Airmail* (1932) (Universal): Slim Summerville, Frank Albertson, Francis Ford, James Flavin, Ward Bond, Harry Tenbrook, James Donlan, Harry Strang, Jack Pennick.

*Flesh* (1932) (M-G-M): Ward Bond.

*Pilgrimage* (1933) (Fox): Charley Grapewin, Francis Ford, Jack Pennick, Ruth Clifford, Si Jenks, Harry Tenbrook, James Donlan, Mary Gordon.

*Doctor Bull* (1933) (Fox): Will Rogers, Andy Devine, Berton Churchill, Francis Ford, Si Jenks, Mary Gordon, James Donlan.

*The Lost Patrol* (1934) (Fox): Victor McLaglen, Wallace Ford, J.M. Kerrigan, Brandon Hurst, Frank Baker, Francis Ford.

*The World Moves On* (1934) (Fox): Stepin Fetchit, Russell Simpson, Jack Pennick, Ben Hall, Francis Ford, Mary Gordon, Harry Tenbrook.

*Judge Priest* (1934) (Fox): Will Rogers, Berton Churchill, Stepin Fetchit, Roger Imhof, Charley Grapewin, Francis Ford, Louis Mason, Vester Pegg, Duke R. Lee, Harry Tenbrook.

*The Whole Town's Talking* (1935) (Columbia): Wallace Ford, Donald Meek, J. Farrell MacDonald, Mary Gordon, Robert Homans, Ed Jones, Francis Ford, James Donlan, Joe Sawyer, Harry Tenbrook, Steve Pendleton.

*The Informer* (1935) (RKO): Victor McLaglen, Wallace Ford, J.M. Kerrigan, Donald Meek, Francis Ford, J. Farrell MacDonald, Joe Sawyer, Sam Harris, Earle Foxe, Frank Baker, Steve Pendleton, Robert Homans, Pat Somerset, Harry Tenbrook.

*Steamboat Round the Bend* (1935) (20th Century-Fox): Will Rogers, Berton Churchill, Francis Ford, Stepin Fetchit, Ed Jones, Roger Imhof, Ben Hall, Si Jenks, Robert Homans, Jack Pennick, James Marcus, Louis Mason, Vester Pegg, Frank Baker.

*The Prisoner of Shark Island* (1936) (20th Century-Fox): Harry Carey, Francis Ford, John Carradine, Duke R. Lee, Robert Homans, James Marcus, Jack Pennick, J.M. Kerrigan, Vester Pegg, Harry Strang, Frank Baker.

*Mary of Scotland* (1936) (20th Century-Fox): John Carradine, Donald Crisp, Alan Mowbray, Mary Gordon, Brandon Hurst, Frank Baker, Earle Foxe, Robert Homans, Lionel Pape, Pat Somerset, Harry Tenbrook.

*The Plough and the Stars* (1936) (20th Century-Fox): Barry Fitzgerald, Arthur Shields, Brandon Hurst, J.M. Kerrigan, Robert

Homans, Mary Gordon, Jack Pennick, Lionel Pape, Francis Ford, Harry Tenbrook, Ben Hall, Steve Pendleton, Frank Baker.

*Wee Willie Winkie* (1937) (20th Century-Fox): Victor McLaglen, Brandon Hurst, Harry Tenbrook, Lionel Pape, Noble Johnson, Jack Pennick, Pat Somerset.

*The Hurricane* (1937) (Goldwyn-United Artists): Thomas Mitchell, John Carradine, Spencer Charters, Chris-Pin Martin.

*Four Men and a Prayer* (1938) (20th Century-Fox): William Henry, John Carradine, Berton Churchill, Barry Fitzgerald, Frank Baker, Brandon Hurst, Robert Lowery, Ruth Clifford, Chris-Pin Martin, Noble Johnson, Mimi Doyle.

*Submarine Patrol* (1938) (20th Century-Fox): Slim Summerville, John Carradine, Warren Hymer, J. Farrell MacDonald, Ward Bond, Jack Pennick, Robert Lowery, Charles Trowbridge, Charles Tannen, Harry Tenbrook, Harry Strang.

*Stagecoach* (1939) (Wanger-United Artists): John Wayne, Thomas Mitchell, John Carradine, Andy Devine, Donald Meek, Berton Churchill, Tom Tyler, Francis Ford, Harry Tenbrook, Jack Pennick, Vester Pegg, Chris-Pin Martin, Louis Mason, Frank Baker, Chief John Big Tree, Duke R. Lee, Robert Homans, Dan Borzage, Hank Worden, Si Jenks..

*Young Mr. Lincoln* (1939) (Cosmopolitian-20th Century-Fox): Henry Fonda, Ward Bond, Donald Meek, Francis Ford, Russell Simpson, Milburn Stone, Charles Halton, Spencer Charters, Charles Tannen, Louis Mason, Robert Lowery, Robert Homans, Harry Tyler, Jack Pennick.

*Drums Along the Mohawk* (1939) (20th Century-Fox): Henry Fonda, John Carradine, Arthur Shields, Ward Bond, Roger Imhof, Francis Ford, Chief John Big Tree, Spencer Charters, Si Jenks, Charles Tannen, Robert Lowery, Jack Pennick, Elizabeth "Tiny"

Jones, Russell Simpson, Lionel Pape, Tom Tyler, Noble Johnson, Frank Baker, Mae Marsh, Ruth Clifford.

*The Grapes of Wrath* (1940) (20th Century-Fox): Henry Fonda, Jane Darwell, John Carradine, Charley Grapewin, Russell Simpson, O.Z. Whitehead, John Qualen, Louis Mason, Ward Bond, Harry Tyler, Roger Imhof, Jack Pennick, Robert Homans, James Flavin, Tom Tyler, Ben Hall, Harry Tenbrook, Charles Tannen, Joe Sawyer, Steve Pendleton, Mae Marsh, Francis Ford, Harry Strang.

*The Long Voyage Home* (1940) (Argosy-Wanger-United Artists): Thomas Mitchell, John Wayne, Barry Fitzgerald, Mildred Natwick, John Qualen, Ward Bond, Arthur Shields, J.M. Kerrigan, Joe Sawyer, Jack Pennick, Dan Borzage, Lionel Pape, Harry Tenbrook, James Flavin.

*Tobacco Road* (1941) (20th Century-Fox): Charley Grapewin, Slim Summerville, Ward Bond, Russell Simpson, Harry Tyler, Spencer Charters, Jack Pennick, Charles Halton, Francis Ford.

*Sex Hygiene* (1941) (Auto Productions-U.S. Army Signal Corps): Charles Trowbridge, Robert Lowery, Charles Tannen.

*How Green Was My Valley* (1941) (20th Century-Fox): Maureen O'Hara, Donald Crisp, Anna Lee, Barry Fitzgerald, Arthur Shields, Lionel Pape, Irving Pichel, Mae Marsh, Elizabeth "Tiny" Jones, Lionel Pape, Ruth Clifford, Frank Baker, Mary Gordon, Ben Hall, Jack Pennick.

*The Battle of Midway* (1942) (U.S. Navy-20th Century-Fox): Henry Fonda, Jane Darwell, Donald Crisp, Irving Pichel.

*December 7th* (1943) (U.S. Navy): George O'Brien, Irving Pichel, Robert Lowery.

*They Were Expendable* (1945) (M-G-M): John Wayne, Ward Bond, Russell Simpson, Arthur Walsh, Harry Tenbrook, Jack

Pennick, Charles Trowbridge, Frank McGrath, Dan Borzage, Tom Tyler, Robert Homans.

*My Darling Clementine* (1946) (20th Century-Fox): Henry Fonda, Ward Bond, Alan Mowbray, Grant Withers, Jane Darwell, J. Farrell MacDonald, Ben Hall, Arthur Walsh, Russell Simpson, Francis Ford, Jack Pennick, Mickey Simpson, Fred Libby, Earle Foxe, Dan Borzage, Duke R. Lee, Mae Marsh.

*The Fugitive* (1947) (Argosy Pictures-RKO): Henry Fonda, Pedro Armendariz, Ward Bond, John Qualen, Chris-Pin Martin, Jack Pennick.

*Fort Apache* (1948) (Argosy Pictures-M-G-M): John Wayne, Henry Fonda, Ward Bond, George O'Brien, Victor McLaglen, Anna Lee, Grant Withers, Jack Pennick, Pedro Armendariz, Mae Marsh, Mickey Simpson, Francis Ford, Hank Worden, Harry Tenbrook, Mary Gordon, Fred Graham, Frank McGrath, Ben Johnson, Frank Baker, Cliff Lyons.

*3 Godfathers* (1948) (Argosy Pictures-M-G-M): John Wayne, Harry Carey Jr., Pedro Armendariz, Ward Bond, Mildred Natwick, Jane Darwell, Mae Marsh, Hank Worden, Fred Libby, Ben Johnson, Jack Pennick, Francis Ford, Ruth Clifford, Cliff Lyons, Harry Tenbrook, Charles Halton, Frank McGrath.

*She Wore a Yellow Ribbon* (1949) (Argosy Pictures-RKO): John Wayne, Ben Johnson, Harry Carey Jr., Victor McLaglen, Mildred Natwick, George O'Brien, Arthur Shields, Francis Ford, Chief John Big Tree, Cliff Lyons, Tom Tyler, Irving Pichel, Noble Johnson, Mickey Simpson, Fred Graham, Frank McGrath, Fred Libby, Jack Pennick, Bill Gettinger/Bill Steel, Fred Kennedy, Peter Ortiz, Chuck Hayward.

*When Willie Comes Marching Home* (1950) (20th Century-Fox): Mae Marsh, Jack Pennick, Mickey Simpson, Harry Tenbrook, Hank Worden, James Flavin, Charles Trowbridge, J.

Farrell MacDonald, Sam Harris, Frank Baker, Charles Halton, Vera Miles, Arthur Walsh, Peter Ortiz, Fred Libby, Harry Strang, Mimi Doyle, Fred Graham.

*Wagon Master* (1950) (Argosy Pictures-RKO): Ben Johnson, Harry Carey Jr., Ward Bond, Jane Darwell, Alan Mowbray, Ruth Clifford, Russell Simpson, Fred Libby, Hank Worden, Mickey Simpson, Francis Ford, Cliff Lyons, Chuck Hayward, Dan Borzage, Frank McGrath, Fred Kennedy.

*Rio Grande* (1950) (Argosy Pictures-Republic): John Wayne, Maureen O'Hara, Ben Johnson, Harry Carey Jr., Victor McLaglen, Grant Withers, Peter Ortiz, Steve Pendleton, Fred Kennedy, Chuck Roberson, Ken Curtis, Shug Fisher, Jack Pennick, Cliff Lyons, Patrick Wayne, Frank McGrath, Chuck Hayward.

*This is Korea!* (1951) (U.S. Navy-Republic): Irving Pichel, George O'Brien, Ward Bond.

*What Price Glory* (1952) (20th Century-Fox): Fred Libby, Dan Borzage, William Henry, Jack Pennick, Tom Tyler, Mickey Simpson, Peter Ortiz, Charles Fitzsimons, James Lilburn, Sean McClory, Fred Kennedy.

*The Quiet Man* (1952) (Argosy Pictures-Republic): John Wayne, Maureen O'Hara, Barry Fitzgerald, Ward Bond, Victor McLaglen, Mildred Natwick, Arthur Shields, Jack MacGowran, Charles Fitzsimons, Sean McClory, Francis Ford, Ken Curtis, Mae Marsh, Harry Tenbrook, James Lilburn, Sam Harris, Harry Tyler, Elizabeth "Tiny" Jones, Patrick Wayne, Ruth Clifford, Fred Kennedy, Mimi Doyle, Frank Baker.

*The Sun Shines Bright* (1953) (Argosy Pictures-Republic): Stepin Fetchit, Russell Simpson, Francis Ford, Grant Withers, Milburn Stone, Jane Darwell, Mae Marsh, Jack Pennick, Chuck Hayward, Mimi Doyle, Patrick Wayne.

*The Bamboo Cross* episode from television's *Jane Wyman Presents* "The Fireside Theatre" episode (1955): Frank Baker.

*Rookie of the Year* episode from television's *Screen Directors Playhouse* series (1955): John Wayne, Vera Miles, Ward Bond, Patrick Wayne, Willis Bouchey, Harry Tyler.

*The Long Gray Line* (1955) (Columbia-Rota): Maureen O'Hara, Donald Crisp, Ward Bond, Harry Carey Jr., Patrick Wayne, Willis Bouchey, Ken Curtis, Milburn Stone, Jack Pennick, Mickey Simpson, James Lilburn, Sean McClory, Mimi Doyle, Harry Tenbrook.

*Mister Roberts* (1955) (Orange Productions-Warner Bros.): Henry Fonda, Ward Bond, Harry Carey Jr., Ken Curtis, William Henry, Harry Tenbrook, Patrick Wayne, Shug Fisher, Dan Borzage, James Flavin, Mimi Doyle, Jack Pennick.

*The Searchers* (1956) (C.V. Whitney-Warner Brothers): John Wayne, Jeffrey Hunter, Vera Miles, Ward Bond, Olive Carey, John Qualen, Ken Curtis, Harry Carey Jr., Hank Worden, Patrick Wayne, Jack Pennick, Bill Gettinger/Bill Steel, Cliff Lyons, Chuck Roberson, Ruth Clifford, Mae Marsh, Dan Borzage, Chuck Hayward, Fred Kennedy, Frank McGrath.

*The Rising of the Moon* (1957) (Four Province Productions-Warner Bros.): Jack MacGowran.

*The Wings of Eagles* (1957) (M-G-M): John Wayne, Maureen O'Hara, Ward Bond, Ken Curtis, Willis Bouchey, Peter Ortiz, Dan Borzage, Jack Pennick, William Henry, Charles Trowbridge, Mae Marsh, Fred Graham, Sam Harris, Chuck Roberson, James Flavin, Olive Carey, Cliff Lyons, Harry Strang, Frank McGrath, Chuck Hayward.

*The Growler Story* (1957) (U.S. Navy): Ward Bond, Ken Curtis.

*The Last Hurrah* (1958) (Columbia): Jeffrey Hunter, Donald Crisp, John Carradine, Willis Bouchey, Wallace Ford, Anna Lee,

Jane Darwell, Frank Albertson, Charles Fitzsimons, Carleton Young, Ken Curtis, O.Z. Whitehead, Arthur Walsh, Dan Borzage, James Flavin, Ruth Clifford, Jack Pennick, Harry Tenbrook, William Henry, Mae Marsh, Harry Tyler, Charles Trowbridge, Fred Kennedy, Sam Harris, Harry Strang, Mimi Doyle, Frank Baker.

*Gideon of Scotland Yard* (1958) (Columbia-British Productions): Anna Lee.

*The Horse Soldiers* (1959) (Mirisch Company-United Artists): John Wayne, Hoot Gibson, Anna Lee, Russell Simpson, Carleton Young, Willis Bouchey, Ken Curtis, O.Z. Whitehead, Hank Worden, Denver Pyle, Jack Pennick, Fred Graham, Chuck Hayward, Sam Harris, William Henry, Cliff Lyons, Dan Borzage, Fred Kennedy.

*Sergeant Rutledge* (1960) (Ford Productions-Warner Bros.): Woody Strode, Jeffrey Hunter, Willis Bouchey, Carleton Young, William Henry, Chuck Hayward, Mae Marsh, Fred Libby, Cliff Lyons, Jack Pennick, Chuck Roberson, Shug Fisher, Hank Worden, Sam Harris.

*The Colter Craven Story* episode from television's *Wagon Train* series (1960): Ward Bond, Carleton Young, Frank McGrath, John Carradine, Chuck Hayward, Ken Curtis, Anna Lee, Cliff Lyons, Willis Bouchey, Mae Marsh, Jack Pennick, Hank Worden, William Henry, Dan Borzage, Chuck Roberson, John Wayne.

*Two Rode Together* (1961) (Ford-Sheptner Productions-Columbia): James Stewart, Andy Devine, Willis Bouchley, Harry Carey Jr., Ken Curtis, Anna Lee, John Qualen, Wood Strode, O.Z. Whitehead, Cliff Lyons, Olive Carey, Mae March, Frank Baker, Ruth Clifford, Sam Harris, Jack Pennick, Chuck Roberson, William Henry, Dan Borzage, Chuck Hayward.

*The Man Who Shot Liberty Valance* (1962) (Ford Productions-Paramount): James Stewart, John Wayne, Vera Miles, Andy Devine, John Carradine, John Qualen, Willis Bouchey, Carleton Young, Woody Strode, O.Z. Whitehead, Denver Pyle, Jack Pennick, Anna Lee, Shug Fisher, Dan Borzage, Chuck Hayward, Chuck Roberson, William Henry, Sam Harris, Frank Baker.

*How the West Was Won*, "The Civil War" segment (1962) (Cinerama-M-G-M): Andy Devine, Willis Bouchey, John Wayne, Ken Curtis, Jack Pennick, Chuck Roberson.

*Flashing Spikes* episode from television's *Alcoa Premiere* series (1962): James Stewart, Patrick Wayne, Carleton Young, Willis Bouchey, Harry Carey Jr., William Henry, John Wayne.

*Donovan's Reef* (1963) (Ford Productions-Paramount): John Wayne, Frank Baker, Patrick Wayne, Mike Mazurki, John Qualen, Chuck Roberson, Mae Marsh, Sam Harris, Cliff Lyons.

*Cheyenne Autumn* (1964) (Ford-Smith Productions-Warner Bros.): James Stewart, Patrick Wayne, John Carradine, Carleton Young, Mike Mazurki, William Henry, George O'Brien, Ken Curtis, Denver Pyle, Shug Fisher, Chuck Roberson, Harry Carey Jr., Ben Johnson, James Flavin, Chuck Hayward, James Lilburn, Sean McClory, Dan Borzage, Harry Strang, Willis Bouchey, John Qualen, Mae Marsh, Cliff Lyons, Sam Harris.

*Young Cassidy* (1965) (Sextant Films-M-G-M): Jack MacGowran

*7 Women* (1966) (Ford-Smith Productions-M-G-M): Anna Lee, Woody Strode, Mike Mazurki, Cliff Lyons, Chuck Roberson, Chuck Hayward.

# One Hundred Twelve
# John Ford Stock Company
# Members and their Ford Films,
# Documentaries,
# and Television Episodes

**Frank Albertson (6)**

*Salute* (1929)

*Men Without Women* (1930)

*Born Reckless* (1930)

*The Brat* (1931)

*Airmail* (1932)

*The Last Hurrah* (1958)

**Pedro Armendariz (3)**

*The Fugitive* (1947)

*Fort Apache* (1948)

*3 Godfathers* (1948)

**Frank Baker (27)**

*Cameo Kirby* (1923)

*Hearts of Oak* (1924)

*The Fighting Heart* (1925)

*Four Sons* (1928)

*Hangman's House* (1928)

*The Black Watch* (1929)

*Men Without Women* (1930)

*Seas Beneath* (1931)

*Arrowsmith* (1931)

*The Lost Patrol* (1934)

*The Informer* (1935)

*Steamboat Round the Bend* (1935)

*The Prisoner of Shark Island* (1936)

*Mary of Scotland* (1936)

*The Plough and the Stars* (1936)

*Four Men and a Prayer* (1938)

*Stagecoach* (1939)

*Drums Along the Mohawk* (1939)

*How Green Was My Valley* (1941)

*Fort Apache* (1948)

*When Willie Comes Marching Home* (1950)

*The Quiet Man* (1952)

*The Bamboo Cross* episode from television's *Jane Wyman Presents "The Fireside Theatre"* (1955)

*The Last Hurrah* (1958)

*Two Rode Together* (1961)

*The Man Who Shot Liberty Valance* (1962)

*Donovan's Reef* (1963)

## Chief John Big Tree (5)

*A Fight for Love* (1919)

*The Iron Horse* (1924)

*Stagecoach* (1929)

*Drums Along the Mohawk* (1939)

*She Wore a Yellow Ribbon* (1949)

## Ward Bond (28)

*Salute* (1929)

*Born Reckless* (1930)

*Up the River* (1930)

*The Brat* (1931)

*Arrowsmith* (1931)

*Airmail* (1932)

*Flesh* (1932)

*Submarine Patrol* (1938)

*Young Mr. Lincoln* (1939)

*Drums Along the Mohawk* (1939)

*The Grapes of Wrath* (1940)

*The Long Voyage Home* (1940)

*Tobacco Road* (1941)

*They Were Expendable* (1945)

*My Darling Clementine* (1946)

*The Fugitive* (1947)

*Fort Apache* (1948)

*3 Godfathers* (1948)

*Wagon Master* (1950)

*This is Korea!* (1951)

*The Quiet Man* (1952)

*Rookie of the Year* episode from television's *Screen Directors Playhouse* (1955)

*The Long Gray Line* (1955)

*Mister Roberts* (1955)

*The Searchers* (1956)

*The Wings of Eagles* (1957)

*The Growler Story* (1957)

*The Colter Craven Story* episode from television's *Wagon Train* series (1960)

## Dan Borzage (16)

*The Iron Horse* (1924)

*Stagecoach* (1939)

*The Long Voyage Home* (1940)

*They Were Expendable* (1945)

*My Darling Clementine* (1946)

*Wagon Master* (1950)

*What Price Glory* (1952)

*Mister Roberts* (1955)

*The Searchers* (1956)

*The Wings of Eagles* (1957)

*The Last Hurrah* (1958)

*The Horse Soldiers* (1959)

*The Colter Craven Story* episode from television's *Wagon Train* series (1960)

*Two Rode Together* (1961)

*The Man Who Shot Liberty Valance* (1962)

*Cheyenne Autumn* (1964)

## Willis Bouchey (12)

*Rookie of the Year* episode from television's *Screen Directors Playhouse* (1955)

*The Long Gray Line* (1955)

*The Wings of Eagles* (1957)

*The Last Hurrah* (1958)

*The Horse Soldiers* (1959)

*Sergeant Rutledge* (1960)

*The Colter Craven Story* episode from television's *Wagon Train* series (1960)

*Two Rode Together* (1961)

*The Man Who Shot Liberty Valance* (1962)

*How the West Was Won*, "The Civil War" segment (1962)

*Flashing Spikes* episode from television's *Alcoa Premier* series (1962)

*Cheyenne Autumn* (1964)

## Frank Campeau (3)

*North of Hudson Bay* (1923)

*Hoodman Blind* (1923)

*3 Bad Men* (1926)

## Harry Carey (26)

*The Soul Herder* (1917)

*Cheyenne's Pal* (1917)

*Straight Shooting* (1917)

*The Secret Man* (1917)

*A Marked Man* (1917)

*Bucking Broadway* (1917)

*The Phantom Riders* (1918)

*Wild Women* (1918)

*Thieves' Gold* (1918)

*The Scarlet Drop* (1918)

*Hell Bent* (1918)

*A Woman's Fool* (1918)

*Three Mounted Men* (1918)

*Roped* (1919)

*A Fight for Love* (1919)

*Bare Fists* (1919)

*Riders of Vengeance* (1919)

*The Outcasts of Poker Flat* (1919)

*The Ace of the Saddle* (1919)

*The Rider of the Law* (1919)

*A Gun Fightin' Gentleman* (1919)

*Marked Men* (1919)

*The Freeze-Out* (1921)

*The Wallop* (1921)

*Desperate Trails* (1921)

*The Prisoner of Shark Island* (1936)

## Harry Carey Jr. (10)

*3 Godfathers* (1948)

*She Wore a Yellow Ribbon* (1949)

*Wagon Master* (1950)

*Rio Grande* (1950)

*The Long Gray Line* (1955)

*Mister Roberts* (1955)

*The Searchers* (1956)

*Two Rode Together* (1961)

*Flashing Spikes* episode from television's *Alcoa Premier* series (1962)

*Cheyenne Autumn* (1964)

## Olive Carey (3)

*The Searchers* (1956)

*The Wings of Eagles* (1957)

*Two Rode Together* (1961)

## John Carradine (12)

*The Prisoner of Shark Island* (1936)

*Mary of Scotland* (1936)

*The Hurricane* (1936)

*Four Men and a Prayer* (1938)

*Submarine Patrol* (1938)

*Stagecoach* (1939)

*Drums Along the Mohawk* (1939)

*The Grapes of Wrath* (1940)

*The Last Hurrah* (1958)

*The Colter Craven Story* episode from television's *Wagon Train* series (1960)

*The Man Who Shot Liberty Valance* (1962)

*Cheyenne Autumn* (1964)

## Spencer Charters (4)

*The Hurricane* (1936)

*Young Mr. Lincoln* (1939)

*Drums Along the Mohawk* (1939)

*Tobacco Road* (1941)

## Berton Churchill (5)

*Doctor Bull* (1933)

*Judge Priest* (1934)

*Steamboat Round the Bend* (1935)

*Four Men and a Prayer* (1938)

*Stagecoach* (1939)

**Ruth Clifford (11)**

*The Face on the Bar Room Floor* (1923)

*Pilgrimage* (1933)

*Four Men and a Prayer* (1938)

*Drums Along the Mohawk* (1939)

*How Green Was My Valley* (1941)

*3 Godfathers* (1948)

*Wagon Master* (1950)

*The Quiet Man* (1952)

*The Searchers* (1956)

*The Last Hurrah* (1958)

*Two Rode Together* (1961)

**Donald Crisp (5)**

*Mary of Scotland* (1936)

*How Green Was My Valley* (1941)

*The Battle of Midway* (1942)

*The Long Gray Line* (1955)

*The Last Hurrah* (1958)

**Ken Curtis (13)**

*Rio Grande* (1950)

*The Quiet Man* (1952)

*The Long Gray Line* (1955)

*Mister Roberts* (1955)

*The Searchers* (1956)

*The Wings of Eagles* (1957)

*The Growler Story* (1957)

*The Last Hurrah* (1958)

*The Horse Soldiers* (1959)

*The Colter Craven Story* episode from television's

*Wagon Train* series (1960)
*Two Rode Together* (1961)
*How the West Was Won*, "The Civil War" segment (1962)
*Cheyenne Autumn* (1964)

**Jane Darwell (7)**

*The Grapes of Wrath* (1940)
*The Battle of Midway* (1942)
*My Darling Clementine* (1946)
*3 Godfathers* (1948)
*Wagon Master* (1950)
*The Sun Shines Bright* (1953)
*The Last Hurrah* (1958)

**Andy Devine (5)**

*Doctor Bull* (1933)
*Stagecoach* (1939)
*Two Rode Together* (1961)
*The Man Who Shot Liberty Valance* (1962)
*How the West Was Won*, "The Civil War" segment (1962)

**James Donlan (4)**

*Airmail* (1932)
*Pilgrimage* (1933)
*Doctor Bull* (1933)
*The Whole Town's Talking* (1935)

**Mimi Doyle (7)**

>*Four Men and a Prayer* (1938)
>
>*When Willie Comes Marching Home* (1950)
>
>*The Quiet Man* (1952)
>
>*The Sun Shines Bright* (1953)
>
>*The Long Gray Line* (1955)
>
>*Mister Roberts* (1955)
>
>*The Last Hurrah* (1958)

**Stepin Fetchit (5)**

>*Salute* (1929)
>
>*The World Moves On* (1934)
>
>*Judge Priest* (1934)
>
>*Steamboat Round the Bend* (1934)
>
>*The Sun Shines Bright* (1953)

**Shug Fisher (5)**

>*Rio Grande* (1950)
>
>*Mister Roberts* (1955)
>
>*Sergeant Rutledge* (1960)
>
>*The Man Who Shot Liberty Valance* (1961)
>
>*Cheyenne Autumn* (1964)

**Barry Fitzgerald (5)**

>*The Plough and the Stars* (1936)
>
>*Four Men and a Prayer* (1938)
>
>*The Long Voyage Home* (1940)
>
>*How Green Was My Valley* (1941)
>
>*The Quiet Man* (1952)

## Charles Fitzsimons (3)

*What Price Glory* (1952)
*The Quiet Man* (1952)
*The Last Hurrah* (1958)

## James Flavin (8)

*Airmail* (1932)
*The Grapes of Wrath* (1940)
*The Long Voyage Home* (1940)
*When Willie Comes Marching Home* (1950)
*Mister Roberts* (1955)
*The Wings of Eagles* (1957)
*The Last Hurrah* (1958)
*Cheyenne Autumn* (1964)

## Henry Fonda (8)

*Young Mr. Lincoln* (1939)
*Drums Along the Mohawk* (1939)
*The Grapes of Wrath* (1940)
*The Battle of Midway* (1942)
*My Darling Clementine* (1946)
*The Fugitive* (1947)
*Fort Apache* (1948)
*Mister Roberts* (1955)

## Francis Ford (31)

*Action* (1921)
*The Village Blacksmith* (1922)
*Three Jumps Ahead* (1923)
*Hearts of Oak* (1924)
*The Fighting Heart* (1925)

*Upstream* (1927)

*The Black Watch* (1929)

*Seas Beneath* (1931)

*Airmail* (1932)

*Pilgrimage* (1933)

*Doctor Bull* (1933)

*The Lost Patrol* (1934)

*The World Moves On* (1934)

*Judge Priest* (1934)

*The Whole Town's Talking* (1935)

*The Informer* (1935)

*Steamboat Round the Bend* (1935)

*The Prisoner of Shark Island* (1936)

*The Plough and the Stars* (1936)

*Stagecoach* (1939)

*Young Mr. Lincoln* (1939)

*Drums Along the Mohawk* (1939)

*The Grapes of Wrath* (1940)

*Tobacco Road* (1941)

*My Darling Clementine* (1946)

*Fort Apache* (1948)

*3 Godfathers* (1948)

*She Wore a Yellow Ribbon* (1949)

*Wagon Master* (1950)

*The Quiet Man* (1952)

*The Sun Shines Bright* (1953)

## Wallace Ford (4)

*The Lost Patrol* (1934)

*The Whole Town's Talking* (1935)

*The Informer* (1935)

*The Last Hurrah* (1958)

**Earle Foxe (6)**

*Upstream* (1927)
*Hangman's House* (1928)
*Four Sons* (1928)
*The Informer* (1935)
*Mary of Scotland* (1936)
*My Darling Clementine* (1946)

**Neva Gerber (4)**

*Hell Bent* (1918)
*Three Mounted Men* (1918)
*Roped* (1919)
*A Fight for Love* (1919)

**Bill Gettinger/Bill Steel (9)**

*The Soul Herder* (1917)
*Cheyenne's Pal* (1917)
*The Secret Man* (1917)
*A Marked Man* (1917)
*Bucking Broadway* (1917)
*The Phantom Riders* (1917)
*The Wallop* (1921)
*She Wore a Yellow Ribbon* (1949)
*The Searchers* (1956)

**Hoot Gibson (13)**

*The Soul Herder* (1917)
*Cheyenne's Pal* (1917)
*Straight Shooting* (1917)

*The Secret Man* (1917)

*A Marked Man* (1917)

*The Fighting Brothers* (1919)

*By Indian Post* (1919)

*The Rustlers* (1919)

*Gun Law* (1919)

*The Gun Packer* (1919)

*Action* (1921)

*Sure Fire* (1921)

*The Horse Soldiers* (1959)

## Mary Gordon (10)

*Hangman's House* (1928)

*The Black Watch* (1929)

*Pilgrimage* (1933)

*Doctor Bull* (1933)

*The World Moves On* (1934)

*The Whole Town's Talking* (1935)

*Mary of Scotland* (1936)

*The Plough and the Stars* (1936)

*How Green Was My Valley* (1941)

*Fort Apache* (1948)

## Fred Graham (5)

*Fort Apache* (1948)

*She Wore a Yellow Ribbon* (1949)

*When Willie Comes Marching Home* (1950)

*The Wings of Eagles* (1957)

*The Horse Soldiers* (1959)

## Charley Grapewin (4)

*Pilgrimage* (1933)

*Judge Priest* (1934)

*The Grapes of Wrath* (1940)

*Tobacco Road* (1941)

## Ben Hall (8)

*Salute* (1929)

*Seas Beneath* (1931)

*The World Moves On* (1934)

*Steamboat Round the Bend* (1935)

*The Plough and the Stars* (1936)

*The Grapes of Wrath* (1940)

*How Green Was My Valley* (1941)

*My Darling Clementine* (1946)

## Charles Halton (4)

*Young Mr. Lincoln* (1939)

*Tobacco Road* (1941)

*3 Godfathers* (1948)

*When Willie Comes Marching Home* (1950)

## Joe Harris (14)

*Hell Bent* (1918)

*Three Mounted Men* (1918)

*A Fight for Love* (1919)

*Bare Fists* (1919)

*Riders of Vengeance* (1919)

*The Outcasts of Poker Flat* (1919)

*The Ace of the Saddle* (1919)

*The Rider of the Law* (1919)

*A Gun Fightin' Gentleman* (1919)

*Marked Men* (1919)
*Hitchin' Posts* (1920)
*The Freeze-Out* (1920)
*The Wallop* (1920)
*Sure Fire* (1921)

**Sam Harris (11)**

*The Informer* (1935)
*When Willie Comes Marching Home* (1950)
*The Quiet Man* (1952)
*The Wings of Eagles* (1957)
*The Last Hurrah* (1958)
*The Horse Soldiers* (1959)
*Sergeant Rutledge* (1960)
*Two Rode Together* (1961)
*The Man Who Shot Liberty Valance* (1962)
*Donovan's Reef* (1963)
*Cheyenne's Autumn* (1964)

**Chuck Hayward (13)**

*She Wore a Yellow Ribbon* (1949)
*Wagon Master* (1950)
*Rio Grande* (1950)
*The Sun Shines Bright* (1953)
*The Searchers* (1956)
*The Wings of Eagles* (1957)
*The Horse Soldiers* (1959)
*Sergeant Rutledge* (1960)
*The Colter Craven Story* episode from television's
*Wagon Train* series (1960)
*Two Rode Together* (1961)

*The Man Who Shot Liberty Valance* (1962)
*Cheyenne Autumn* (1964)
*7 Women* (1966)

## William Henry (12)

*Four Men and a Prayer* (1938)
*What Price Glory* (1952)
*Mister Roberts* (1955)
*The Wings of Eagles* (1957)
*The Last Hurrah* (1958)
*The Horse Soldiers* (1959)
*Sergeant Rutledge* (1960)
*The Colter Craven Story* episode from television's *Wagon Train* series (1960)
*Two Rode Together* (1961)
*The Man Who Shot Liberty Valance* (1962)
*Flashing Spikes* episode from television's *Alcoa Premier* series (1962)
*Cheyenne Autumn* (1964)

## Robert Homans (11)

*Born Reckless* (1930)
*The Whole Town's Talking* (1935)
*The Informer* (1935)
*Steamboat Round the Bend* (1935)
*The Prisoner of Shark Island* (1936)
*Mary of Scotland* (1936)
*The Plough and the Stars* (1936)
*Stagecoach* (1939)
*Young Mr. Lincoln* (1939)
*The Grapes of Wrath* (1940)

*They Were Expendable* (1945)

**Jeffrey Hunter (3)**

> *The Searchers* (1955)
> *The Last Hurrah* (1958)
> *Sergeant Rutledge* (1960)

**Brandon Hurst (7)**

> *Lightnin'* (1925)
> *The Shamrock Handicap* (1926)
> *The Lost Patrol* (1934)
> *Mary of Scotland* (1936)
> *The Plough and the Stars* (1936)
> *Wee Willie Winkie* (1937)
> *Four Men and a Prayer* (1938)

**Warren Hymer (5)**

> *Men Without Women* (1930)
> *Born Reckless* (1930)
> *Up The River* (1930)
> *Seas Beneath* (1931)
> *Submarine Patrol* (1938)

**Roger Imhof (4)**

> *Judge Priest* (1934)
> *Steamboat Round the Bend* (1935)
> *Drums Along the Mohawk* (1939)
> *The Grapes of Wrath* (1940)

**Si Jenks (6)**

*The Village Blacksmith* (1922)

*Pilgrimage* (1933)

*Doctor Bull* (1933)

*Steamboat Round the Bend* (1935)

*Stagecoach* (1939)

*Drums Along the Mohawk* (1939)

**Ben Johnson (6)**

*Fort Apache* (1948)

*3 Godfathers* (1948)

*She Wore a Yellow Ribbon* (1949)

*Wagon Master* (1950)

*Rio Grande* (1950)

*Cheyenne Autumn* (1964)

**Noble Johnson (5)**

*The Wallop* (1921)

*Wee Willie Winkie* (1937)

*Four Men and a Prayer* (1938)

*Drums Along the Mohawk* (1939)

*She Wore a Yellow Ribbon* (1949)

**Ed Jones (13)**

*Cheyenne's Pal* (1917)

*Wild Women* (1918)

*A Woman's Fool* (1918)

*By Indian Post* (1919)

*Gun Law* (1919)

*The Gun Packer* (1919)

*The Last Outlaw* (1919)

*The Ace of the Saddle* (1919)

*The Big Punch* (1921)

*Action* (1921)

*The Iron Horse* (1924)

*The Whole Town's Talking* (1935)

*Steamboat Round the Bend* (1935)

## Elizabeth "Tiny" Jones (4)

*The Iron Horse* (1924)

*Drums Along the Mohawk* (1939)

*How Green Was My Valley* (1941)

*The Quiet Man* (1952)

## Fred Kennedy (8)

*She Wore a Yellow Ribbon* (1949)

*Wagon Master* (1950)

*Rio Grande* (1950)

*What Price Glory* (1952)

*The Quiet Man* (1952)

*The Searchers* (1956)

*The Last Hurrah* (1958)

*The Horse Soldiers* (1959)

## J.M. Kerrigan (5)

*The Lost Patrol* (1934)

*The Informer* (1935)

*The Prisoner of Shark Island* (1936)

*The Plough and the Stars* (1936)

*The Long Voyage Home* (1940)

## Anna Lee (9)

*How Green Was My Valley* (1941)

*Fort Apache* (1948)

*The Last Hurrah* (1958)

*Gideon of Scotland Yard* (1958)

*The Horse Soldiers* (1959)

*The Colter Craven Story* episode from television's *Wagon Train* series (1960)

*Two Rode Together* (1961)

*The Man Who Shot Liberty Valance* (1962)

*7 Women* (1966)

## Duke R. Lee (16)

*The Soul Herder* (1917)

*Straight Shooting* (1917)

*Hell Bent* (1918)

*The Fighting Brothers* (1919)

*By Indian Post* (1919)

*Gun Packer* (1919)

*The Outcast at Poker Flat* (1919)

*The Ace of the Saddle* (1919)

*The Rider of the Law* (1919)

*A Gun Fightin' Gentleman* (1919)

*Hitchin' Posts* (1920)

*Just Pals* (1920)

*Judge Priest* (1934)

*The Prisoner of Shark Island* (1936)

*Stagecoach* (1939)

*My Darling Clementine* (1946)

**Jennie Lee (5)**

> *Riders of Vengeance* (1919)
> *The Rider of the Law* (1919)
> *The Big Punch* (1921)
> *North of Hudson Bay* (1923)
> *Hearts of Oak* (1924)

**Fred Libby (7)**

> *My Darling Clementine* (1946)
> *3 Godfathers* (1948)
> *She Wore a Yellow Ribbon* (1949)
> *When Willie Comes Marching Home* (1950)
> *Wagon Master* (1950)
> *What Price Glory* (1952)
> *Sergeant Rutledge* (1960)

**James Lilburn (4)**

> *What Price Glory* (1953)
> *The Quiet Man* (1952)
> *The Long Gray Line* (1954)
> *Cheyenne Autumn* (1964)

**Robert Lowery (6)**

> *Four Men and a Prayer* (1938)
> *Submarine Patrol* (1938)
> *Young Mr. Lincoln* (1939)
> *Drums Along the Mohawk* (1939)
> *Sex Hygiene* (1941)
> *December 7th* (1943)

## Cliff Lyons (14)

*Fort Apache* (1948)

*3 Godfathers* (1948)

*She Wore a Yellow Ribbon* (1949)

*Wagon Master* (1950)

*Rio Grande* (1950)

*The Searchers* (1956)

*The Wings of Eagles* (1957)

*The Horse Soldiers* (1959)

*Sergeant Rutledge* (1960)

*The Colter Craven Story* episode from television's
*Wagon Train* series (1960)

*Two Rode Together* (1961)

*Donovan's Reef* (1963)

*Cheyenne Autumn* (1964)

*7 Women* (1966)

## Sean McClory (4)

*What Price Glory* (1952)

*The Quiet Man* (1952)

*The Long Gray Line* (1955)

*Cheyenne Autumn* (1964)

## J. Farrell MacDonald (26)

*Roped* (1919)

*A Fight for Love* (1919)

*Riders of Vengeance* (1919)

*The Outcasts of Poker Flat* (1919)

*Marked Men* (1919)

*Hitchin' Posts* (1920)

*The Freeze-Out* (1921)

*The Wallop* (1921)

*Action* (1921)

*The Iron Horse* (1924)

*Lightnin'* (1925)

*Kentucky Pride* (1925)

*The Fighting* Heart (1925)

*Thank You* (1925)

*The Shamrock Handicap* (1926)

*3 Bad Men* (1926)

*Riley the Cop* (1928)

*Strong Boy* (1929)

*Men Without Women* (1930)

*Born Reckless* (1930)

*The Brat* (1931)

*The Whole Town's Talking* (1935)

*The Informer* (1935)

*Submarine Patrol* (1938)

*My Darling Clementine* (1946)

*When Willie Comes Marching Home* (1950)

## Jack MacGowran (3)

*The Quiet Man* (1952)

*The Rising of the Moon* (1957)

*Young Cassidy* (1965)

## Frank McGrath (9)

*They Were Expendable* (1945)

*Fort Apache* (1948)

*3 Godfathers* (1948)

*She Wore a Yellow Ribbon* (1949)

*Wagon Master* (1950)

*Rio Grande* (1950)

*The Searchers* (1956)

*The Wings of Eagles* (1957)

*The Colter Craven Story* episode from television's *Wagon Train* series (1960)

## Victor McLaglen (12)

*The Fighting Heart* (1925)

*Mother Machree* (1926)

*Hangman's House* (1928)

*Strong Boy* (1929)

*The Black Watch* (1929)

*The Lost Patrol* (1934)

*The Informer* (1935)

*Wee Willie Winkie* (1937)

*Fort Apache* (1948)

*She Wore a Yellow Ribbon* (1949)

*Rio Grande* (1950)

*The Quiet Man* (1952)

## Molly Malone (10)

*The Soul Herder* (1917)

*Straight Shooting* (1917)

*A Marked Man* (1917)

*Bucking Broadway* (1917)

*The Phantom Riders* (1918)

*Wild Women* (1918)

*Thieves' Gold* (1918)

*The Scarlet Drop* (1918)

*A Woman's Fool* (1918)

*Sure Fire* (1921)

**James Marcus (6)**

>*The Iron Horse* (1924)
>
>*Lightnin'* (1925)
>
>*The Fighting Heart* (1925)
>
>*Arrowsmith* (1931)
>
>*Steamboat Round the Bend* (1935)
>
>*The Prisoner of Shark Island* (1936)

**Mae Marsh (17)**

>*Drums Along the Mohawk* (1939)
>
>*The Grapes of Wrath* (1940)
>
>*How Green Was My Valley* (1941)
>
>*My Darling Clementine* (1946)
>
>*Fort Apache* (1948)
>
>*3 Godfathers* (1948)
>
>*When Willie Comes Marching Home* (1950)
>
>*The Quiet Man* (1952)
>
>*The Sun Shines Bright* (1953)
>
>*The Searchers* (1956)
>
>*The Wings of Eagles* (1957)
>
>*The Last Hurrah* (1958)
>
>*Sergeant Rutledge* (1960)
>
>*The Colter Craven Story* episode from television's *Wagon Train* series (1960)
>
>*Two Rode Together* (1961)
>
>*Donovan's Reef* (1963)
>
>*Cheyenne Autumn* (1964)

**Chris-Pin Martin (4)**

>*The Hurricane* (1936)
>
>*Four Men and a Prayer* (1938)

*Stagecoach* (1939)
*The Fugitive* (1947)

**Louis Mason (5)**

*Judge Priest* (1934)
*Steamboat Round the Bend* (1935)
*Stagecoach* (1939)
*Young Mr. Lincoln* (1939)
*The Grapes of Wrath* (1940)

**Mike Mazurki (3)**

*Donovan's Reef* (1963)
*Cheyenne Autumn* (1964)
*7 Women* (1966)

**Donald Meek (4)**

*The Whole Town's Talking* (1935)
*The Informer* (1935)
*Stagecoach* (1939)
*Young Mr. Lincoln* (1939)

**Vera Miles (4)**

*When Willie Comes Marching Home* (1950)
*Rookie of the Year* episode from television's *Screen Directors Playhouse* (1955)
*The Searchers* (1956)
*The Man Who Shot Liberty Valance* (1962)

## Thomas Mitchell (3)

*The Hurricane* (1937)

*Stagecoach* (1939)

*The Long Voyage Home* (1940)

## Pete Morrison (5)

*The Fighting Brothers* (1919)

*By Indian Post* (1919)

*The Rustlers* (1919)

*Gun Law* (1919)

*The Gun Packer* (1919)

## Alan Mowbray (3)

*Mary of Scotland* (1936)

*My Darling Clementine* (1946)

*Wagon Master* (1950)

## Mildred Natwick (4)

*The Long Voyage Home* (1940)

*3 Godfathers* (1948)

*She Wore a Yellow Ribbon* (1949)

*The Quiet Man* (1952)

## George O'Brien (12)

*The Iron Horse* (1924)

*The Fighting Heart* (1925)

*Thank You* (1925)

*3 Bad Men* (1926)

*The Blue Eagle* (1926)

*Salute* (1929)

*Seas Beneath* (1931)

*December 7th (*1943)
*Fort Apache* (1948)
*She Wore a Yellow Ribbon* (1949)
*This is Korea!* (1951)
*Cheyenne Autumn* (1964)

## Maureen O'Hara (5)

*How Green Was My Valley* (1941)
*Rio Grande* (1950)
*The Quiet Man* (1952)
*The Long Gray Line* (1955)
*The Wings of Eagles* (1957)

## Peter Ortiz (5)

*She Wore a Yellow Ribbon* (1949)
*When Willie Comes Marching Home* (1950)
*Rio Grande* (1950)
*What Price Glory* (1952)
*The Wings of Eagles* (1957)

## Lionel Pape (6)

*Mary of Scotland* (1936)
*The Plough and the Stars* (1936)
*Wee Willie Winkie* (1937)
*Drums Along the Mohawk* (1939)
*The Long Voyage Home* (1940)
*How Green Was My Valley* (1941)

## Vester Pegg (22)

*The Soul Herder* (1917)
*Cheyenne's Pal* (1917)

*Straight Shooting* (1917)

*The Secret Man* (1917)

*A Marked Man* (1917)

*Bucking Broadway* (1917)

*The Phantom Riders* (1918)

*Wild Women* (1918)

*Thieves' Gold* (1918)

*The Scarlett Drop* (1918)

*Hell Bent* (1918)

*A Woman's Fool* (1918)

*Bare Fists* (1919)

*The Riders of Vengeance* (1919)

*The Outcasts of Poker Flat* (1919)

*The Ace of the Saddle* (1919)

*The Rider of the Law* (1919)

*3 Bad Men* (1926)

*Judge Priest* (1934)

*Steamboat Round the Bend* (1935)

*The Prisoner of Shark Island* (1936)

*Stagecoach* (1939)

## Steve Pendleton (7)

*Up the River* (1930)

*Seas Beneath* (1931)

*The Whole Town's Talking* (1935)

*The Informer* (1935)

*The Plough and the Stars* (1936)

*The Grapes of Wrath* (1940)

*Rio Grande* (1950)

## Jack Pennick (43)

*The Blue Eagle* (1926)

*Four Sons* (1928)

*Hangman's House* (1928)

*Strong Boy* (1929)

*The Black Watch* (1929)

*Salute* (1929)

*Born Reckless* (1930)

*Airmail* (1932)

*Pilgrimage* (1933)

*The World Moves On* (1934)

*Steamboat Round the Bend* (1935)

*The Plough and the Stars* (1936)

*The Prisoner of Shark Island* (1936)

*Wee Willie Winkie* (1937)

*Submarine Patrol* (1938)

*Stagecoach* (1939)

*Drums Along the Mohawk* (1939)

*Young Mr. Lincoln* (1939)

*The Grapes of Wrath* (1940)

*The Long Voyage Home* (1940)

*Tobacco Road* (1941)

*How Green Was My Valley* (1941)

*They Were Expendable* (1945)

*My Darling Clementine* (1946)

*The Fugitive* (1947)

*Fort Apache* (1948)

*3 Godfathers* (1948)

*She Wore a Yellow Ribbon* (1949)

*When Willie Comes Marching Home* (1950)

*Rio Grande* (1950)

*What Price Glory* (1952)
*The Sun Shines Bright* (1953)
*The Long Gray Line* (1955)
*Mister Roberts* (1955)
*The Searchers* (1956)
*The Wings of Eagles* (1957)
*The Last Hurrah* (1958)
*The Horse Soldiers* (1959)
*Sergeant Rutledge* (1960)
*The Colter Craven Story* episode from television's *Wagon Train* series (1960)
*Two Rode Together* (1961)
*The Man Who Shot Liberty Valance* (1962)
*How the West Was Won*, "The Civil War" segment (1962)

**Irving Pichel (5)**

*How Green Was My Valley* (1941)
*The Battle of Midway* (1942)
*December 7th* (1943)
*She Wore a Yellow Ribbon* (1949)
*This is Korea!* (1951)

**Denver Pyle (3)**

*The Horse Soldiers* (1959)
*The Man Who Shot Liberty Valance* (1962)
*Cheyenne Autumn* (1964)

**John Qualen (9)**

*Arrowsmith* (1931)
*The Grapes of Wrath* (1940)

*The Long Voyage Home* (1940)

*The Fugitive* (1947)

*The Searchers* (1956)

*Two Rode Together* (1961)

*The Man Who Shot Liberty Valance* (1962)

*Donovan's Reef* (1963)

*Cheyenne Autumn* (1964)

## Chuck Roberson (11)

*Rio Grande* (1950)

*The Searchers* (1956)

*The Wings of Eagles* (1957)

*Sergeant Rutledge* (1960)

*The Colten Craven Story* episode from television's *Wagon Train* series (1960)

*Two Rode Together* (1961)

*The Man Who Shot Liberty Valance* (1962)

*How the West Was Won*, "The Civil War" segment (1962)

*Donovan's Reef* (1963)

*Cheyenne Autumn* (1964)

*7 Women* (1966)

## Will Rogers (3)

*Doctor Bull* (1933)

*Judge Priest* (1935)

*Steamboat Round the Bend* (1935)

## Joe Sawyer (4)

*The Whole Town's Talking* (1935)

*The Informer* (1935)

*The Long Voyage Home* (1940)
*The Grapes of Wrath* (1940)

**Arthur Shields (6)**

*The Plough and the Stars* (1936)
*Drums Along the Mohawk* (1939)
*The Long Voyage Home* (1940)
*How Green Was My Valley* (1941)
*She Wore a Yellow Ribbon* (1949)
*The Quiet Man* (1952)

**Mickey Simpson (7)**

*My Darling Clementine* (1946)
*Fort Apache* (1948)
*She Wore a Yellow Ribbon* (1949)
*When Willie Comes Marching Home* (1950)
*Wagon Master* (1950)
*What Price Glory* (1952)
*The Long Gray Line* (1955)

**Russell Simpson (10)**

*The World Moves On* (1934)
*Young Mr. Lincoln* (1939)
*Drums Along the Mohawk* (1939)
*The Grapes of Wrath* (1940)
*Tobacco Road* (1941)
*They Were Expendable* (1945)
*My Darling Clementine* (1946)
*Wagon Master* (1950)
*The Sun Shines Bright* (1953)
*The Horse Soldiers* (1959)

**Pat Somerset (9)**

> *Mother Machree* (1928)
>
> *The Black Watch* (1929)
>
> *Men Without Women* (1930)
>
> *Born Reckless* (1930)
>
> *Up the River* (1930)
>
> *Arrowsmith* (1931)
>
> *The Informer* (1935)
>
> *Mary of Scotland* (1936)
>
> *Wee Willie Winkie* (1937)

**James Stewart (4)**

> *Two Rode Together* (1961)
>
> *The Man Who Shot Liberty Valance* (1962)
>
> *Flashing Spikes* episode from television's *Alcoa Premier* series (1962)
>
> *Cheyenne Autumn* (1964)

**Milburn Stone (3)**

> *Young Mr. Lincoln* (1939)
>
> *The Sun Shines Bright* (1953)
>
> *The Long Gray Line* (1955)

**Harry Strang (10)**

> *Born Reckless* (1930)
>
> *Seas Beneath* (1930)
>
> *Airmail* (1932)
>
> *The Prisoner of Shark Island* (1936)
>
> *Submarine Patrol* (1938)
>
> *The Grapes of Wrath* (1940)
>
> *When Willie Comes Marching Home* (1950)

*The Wings of Eagles* (1957)
*The Last Hurrah* (1958)
*Cheyenne Autumn* (1964)

**Woody Strode (4)**

*Sergeant Rutledge* (1960)
*Two Rode Together* (1961)
*The Man Who Shot Liberty Valance* (1962)
*7 Women* (1966)

**Slim Summerville (4)**

*Strong Boy* (1929)
*Airmail* (1932)
*Submarine Patrol* (1938)
*Tobacco Road* (1941)

**Charles Tannen (5)**

*Submarine Patrol* (1938)
*Young Mr. Lincoln* (1939)
*Drums Along the Mohawk* (1939)
*The Grapes of Wrath* (1940)
*Sex Hygiene* (1941)

**Harry Tenbrook (28)**

*Thieves' Gold* (1918)
*The Blue Eagle* (1926)
*Four Sons* (1928)
*Salute* (1929)
*Men Without Women* (1930)
*Born Reckless* (1930)
*Seas Beneath* (1931)

*Airmail* (1932)
*Pilgrimage* (1933)
*The World Moves On* (1934)
*Judge Priest* (1934)
*The Whole Town's Talking* (1935)
*The Informer* (1935)
*Mary of Scotland* (1936)
*The Plough and the Stars* (1936)
*Wee Willie Winkie* (1937)
*Submarine Patrol* (1938)
*Stagecoach* (1939)
*The Grapes of Wrath* (1940)
*The Long Voyage Home* (1940)
*They Were Expendable* (1945)
*Fort Apache* (1948)
*3 Godfathers* (1948)
*When Willie Comes Marching Home* (1950)
*The Quiet Man* (1952)
*The Long Gray Line* (1955)
*Mister Roberts* (1955)
*The Last Hurrah* (1958)

## Charles Trowbridge (6)

*Submarine Patrol* (1938)
*Sex Hygiene* (1941)
*They Were Expendable* (1945)
*When Willie Comes Marching Home* (1950)
*The Wings of Eagles* (1957)
*The Last Hurrah* (1958)

## Harry Tyler (6)

*Young Mr. Lincoln* (1939)
*The Grapes of Wrath* (1940)
*Tobacco Road* (1941)
*The Quiet Man* (1952)
*Rookie of the Year* episode from television's *Screen Directors Playhouse* (1955)
*The Last Hurrah* (1958)

## Tom Tyler (6)

*Stagecoach* (1939)
*Drums Along the Mohawk* (1939)
*The Grapes of Wrath* (1940)
*They Were Expendable* (1945)
*She Wore a Yellow Ribbon* (1949)
*What Price Glory* (1952)

## Arthur Walsh (4)

*They Were Expendable* (1945)
*My Darling Clementine* (1946)
*When Willie Comes Marching Home* (1950)
*The Last Hurrah* (1958)

## John Wayne (24)

*Mother Machree* (1928)
*Four Sons* (1928)
*Hangman's House* (1928)
*The Black Watch* (1929)
*Salute* (1929)
*Men Without Women* (1930)
*Born Reckless* (1930)

*Stagecoach* (1939)

*The Long Voyage Home* (1940)

*They Were Expendable* (1945)

*Fort Apache* (1948)

*3 Godfathers* (1948)

*She Wore a Yellow Ribbon* (1949)

*Rio Grande* (1950)

*The Quiet Man* (1952)

*Rookie of the Year* episode from television's *Screen Directors Playhouse* (1955)

*The Searchers* (1956)

*The Wings of Eagles* (1957)

*The Horse Soldiers* (1959)

*The Colter Craven Story* episode from television's *Wagon Train* series (1960)

*The Man Who Shot Liberty Valance* (1962)

*How the West Was Won*, "The Civil War" segment (1962)

*Flashing Spikes* episode from television's *Alcoa Premier* series (1962)

*Donovan's Reef* (1963)

## Patrick Wayne (10)

*Rio Grande* (1950)

*The Quiet Man* (1952)

*The Sun Shines Bright* (1953)

*Rookie of the Year* episode from television's *Screen Directors Playhouse* (1955)

*The Long Gray Line* (1955)

*Mister Roberts* (1955)

*The Searchers* (1956)

*Flashing Spikes* episode from television's *Alcoa Premier* series (1962)
*Donovan's Reef* (1963)
*Cheyenne Autumn* (1964)

## O.Z. Whitehead (5)

*The Grapes of Wrath* (1940)
*The Last Hurrah* (1958)
*The Horse Soldiers* (1959)
*Two Rode Together* (1961)
*The Man Who Shot Liberty Valance* (1962)

## Grant Withers (5)

*Upstream* (1927)
*My Darling Clementine* (1946)
*Fort Apache* (1948)
*Rio Grande* (1950)
*The Sun Shines Bright* (1953)

## Hank Worden (9)

*Stagecoach* (1939)
*Fort Apache* (1948)
*3 Godfathers* (1948)
*When Willie Comes Marching Home* (1950)
*Wagon Master* (1950)
*The Searchers* (1956)
*The Horse Soldiers* (1959)
*Sergeant Rutledge* (1960)
*The Colter Craven Story* episode from television's *Wagon Train* series (1960)

## Carleton Young (7)

*The Last Hurrah* (1958)

*The Horse Soldiers* (1959)

*Sergeant Rutledge* (1960)

*The Colter Craven Story* episode from television's *Wagon Train* series (1960)

*The Man Who Shot Liberty Valance* (1962)

*Flashing Spikes* episode from television's *Alcoa Premier* series (1962)

*Cheyenne Autumn* (1964)

# Recommended Readings

The following thirty-nine books offer more information about John Ford's stock company. For further listings, please consult my volume, *John Ford: A Bio-Bibliography* (Westport, CT: Greenwood Press, 1998); April Lane's invaluable website, *Directed by John Ford*, and Indiana University's The Lilly Library, where the John Ford Collection is located.

Anderson, Lindsay. *About John Ford*. London: Plexus: 1981.

Bagdanovich, Peter. *John Ford*. Berkeley: University of California Press, 1978.

Basinger, Jeanine. *The Star Machine*. New York: Random House, 2007.

Baxter, John. *The Cinema of John Ford*. New York: A.S. Barnes, 1971.

Blum, Daniel. *A New Pictorial History of the Talkies*. New York: G.P. Putnam Sons, 1968.

Carey Jr., Harry. *Company of Heroes: My Life as an Actor in the John Ford Stock Company*. Metuchen, NJ: Scarecrow Press, 1994.

Darby, William. *John Ford's Westerns: A Thematic Analysis*. Jefferson, NC: McFarland, 1996.

Davis, Ronald. *John Ford: Hollywood's Old Master*. Norman, OK: University of Oklahoma Press, 1995.

Donlan, Yolanda. *Shake the Stars Down*. London: Hodder and Stoughton, 1976.

Eyman, Scott. *Print the Legend: The Life and Times of John Ford*. New York: Simon & Schuster, 1999.

Fonda, Henry and Howard Teichmann. *Fonda: My Life*. New York: NAL Books, 1981.

Ford, Dan. *Pappy: The Life of John Ford*. Englewood Cliffs, NJ: Prentice Hall, 1979.

Frazier, Adrian. *Hollywood Irish: John Ford, Abbey Actors and the Irish Revival in Hollywood*. Dublin: Lilliput Press, 2011.

Gallagher, Tag. *John Ford: The Man and His Films*. Berkeley: University of California Press, 1986.

Juran, Robert. *Old Familiar Faces: The Great Character Actors and Actresses of Hollywood's Golden Era*. Sarasota, FL: Movie Memories Publishing, 1995.

Katz, Ephraim. *The Film Encyclopedia*, Third Edition. Revised by Fred Klein and Ronald Dean Nolan. New York: Harper Perennial, 1998.

McBride, Joseph. *Searching for John Ford: A Life*. New York: St. Martin's Griffin, 2001.

McBride, Joseph and Michael Wilmington. *John Ford*. London: Secker and Warburg, 1975.

Meyers, Warren. *Who is That? The Late Late Viewers Guide to the Old Old Movie Players*. New York: Bell Publishing, 1982.

Miller, Frank. *Leading Men: The 50 Most Unforgettable Actors of the Studio Era*. San Francisco: Chronicle Books, 2006.

O'Brien, Darcy. *A Way of Life, Like No Other*. New York: New York Review Books Classics, 2011.

O'Hara, Maureen. *'Tis Herself: A Memoir*. New York: Simon & Schuster, 2004.

Parish, James Robert. *Hollywood Character Actors*. New Rochelle, NY: Arlington, 1978.

Parrish, Robert. *Growing Up in Hollywood.* New York: Harcourt Brace, 1976.

Parrish, Robert. *Hollywood Doesn't Live Here Anymore.* Boston: Little Brown, 1988.

Place, Janey. *The Non-Western Films of John Ford.* Secaucus, NJ: Citadel Press, 1979.

Place, Janey. *The Western Films of John Ford.* Secaucus, NJ: Citadel Press, 1973.

Quinlan, David. *The Illustrated Encyclopedia of Movie Character Actors,* New York: Harmony, 1985.

Roberson, Chuck. *The Fall Guy: Thirty Years as the Duke's Double.* New York: Universe Books, 1980.

Sarris, Andrew. *The John Ford Movie Mystery.* Bloomington, IN: Indiana University Press, 1975.

Sarvady, Andrea. *Leading Ladies: The 50 Most Unforgettable Actresses of the Studio Era.* San Francisco: Chronicle Books, 2006.

Sinclair, Andrew. *John Ford.* New York: Dial Press/James Wade, 1979.

Slide, Anthony. *Hollywood Unknowns: A History of Extras, Bit Players, and Stand-Ins.* Jackson, MS: University Press of Mississippi, 2012.

Slide, Anthony. *Silent Players: A Biographical and Autobiographical Study of 100 Silent Actors and Actresses.* Lexington, KY: The University Press of Kentucky, 2002.

Strode, Woody and Sam Young. *Goal Dust.* Lanham, MD: Madison Books, 1990.

Twomey, Alfred. *The Versatiles: A Study of Supporting Character Actors and Actresses in the American Motion Picture, 1930-1955.* New York: A.S. Barnes, 1969.

Von Hoffmann, Todd. *The Von Hoffmann Bros.' Bigger Damner Book of Sheer Manliness.* Long Island City, NY: QNY, 2009.

Wills, Gary. *John Wayne: The Politics of Celebrity.* New York: Simon & Schuster, 1997.

Young, Jordan R. *Reel Characters: Great Movie Character Actors.* Beverly Hills, CA: Moonstone: 1986.

# "Two for the Road"

John Ford was a strong-willed artist who was an enigma to many. He could be quite kind, but he could also be cruel and cantankerous. He created his personal realm on his set and in his films, and instilled great loyalty in his company of players. And he was not above being silly:

John Ford and Wallace Beery during the filming of *Flesh* (1932).

.

CPSIA information can be obtained at www.ICGtesting.com
Printed in the USA
BVOW021241220213

313958BV00004B/8/P